JUMBO JACK'S COOKBOOKS
AUDUBON MEDIA CORPORATION
301 BROADWAY • AUDUBON IA 50025
1-800-798-2635

HORMONE HELPER
COOKBOOK

by
Bruce Carlson

The efficaciousness of these recipes to promote hormone production and to thereby, enhance the body's ability in the various areas discussed is based on no less than intellectual imposture, scientific surreptitriousness, and entreperneural equivocation. Anyone who seriously puts any credence in these shoud run, not walk, but run . . . to the nearest post office to send me their name and address. I'll want to chat with you about how I fell heir to the Brooklyn Bridge, and have it for sale at a real bargin.

Bruce Carlson

© 1996 by Bruce Carlson

All rights reserved. No part of this book may be reproduced or transmitted in any form or by any means, electronic or mechanical, including photocopying, recording or by any informational storage or retrieval system, except by a reviewer who may quote brief passages in a review to be printed in a magazine or newspaper-without permission in writing from the publisher.

* * * * * * * * *

Although the author has exhaustively researched all sources to ensure the accuracy and completeness of the information contained in this book, he assumes no responsibility for errors, inaccuracies, ommisions, or any inconsistency herein. Any slights of people or organizations are unintentional. Readers should consult an attorney or accountant for specific applications to their individual publishing ventures.

QUIXOTE PRESS
31798 K18S
Sioux City, IA
51109
1-800-571-BOOK

DEDICATION

-to the Research Staff
who did all the interviews
and all the statistical work
for this book.

TABLE of CONTENTS

Dedication iv
Preface ix
Foreword xi

Recipes for dishes to enhance:

MENTAL PROCESSES

Appetizers & Beverages .	15	Soups & Sandwiches	37
Candy & Cookies	21	Salads	41
Breads	25	Main Dishes	51
Veggies	31	Desserts	61

Recipes for dishes for:

IMPROVEMENT OF MUSCLE TONE

Appetizers & Beverages .	67	Soups & Sandwiches . . .	89
Candy & Cookies	73	Salads	93
Breads	77	Main Dishes	103
Veggies	83	Desserts	113

Recipes for dishes to enhance

DIGESTION of FOOD

Appetizers & Beverages	119	Soups & Sandwiches...	141
Candy & Cookies......	125	Salads..............	145
Breads	129	Main Dishes	155
Veggies..............	135	Desserts	165

Recipes for dishes to enhance

SEX DRIVE

Appetizers & Beverages	173	Soups & Sandwiches...	195
Candy & Cookies......	179	Salads..............	199
Breads	183	Main Dishes	209
Veggies..............	189	Desserts	219

Order Form 224

OK, lets use a little common sense here . . . . We all know how important our hormones are. We all know how they call the shots on what goes on in our bodies.

    They're the heavy hitters
    & can make life pretty
    exciting.

Further, we all know that how our bodies operate depends on what we eat.

Well, these recipes are just plain flat out designed to rev up the hormone production . . . .

    . . . . then . . . . watch out!!

PREFACE

This cookbook features combinations of various foods that have been shown to have effects on the production of various hormones in the human body.

Since hormones are, to an extent, specific to various processes in the body, these recipes can be used to enhance these processes.

The four processes addressed in this book are:

MENTAL PROCESSES
IMPROVEMENT OF MUSCLE TONE
DIGESTION OF FOOD
SEX DRIVE

And, there are recipes listed under each of these four areas that are selected to improve the appropriate hormone production.

x

FOREWORD

Bruce Carlson has asked me to say something nice about this book here on this page.

I'd do that too, if he'd ever pay me for the last time I said something nice about one of his books.

My personal opinion is that he's either been snifing the pickling spice or taking little naps in the kitchen with his head bone too close to the microwave.

> Prof. Phil Hey
> Briar Cliff College
> Sioux City, IA

MENTAL PROCESSES

APPETIZERS & BEVERAGES

FRUIT SLUSH

1 (6 oz.) can frozen lemonade
1 (8 oz.) can frozen orange juice
1 (10 oz.) box frozen strawberries
1 (1 lb.) can crushed pineapple with juice
1 (4 oz.) jar maraschino cherries & juice
3 bananas (diced)
2½ C. water
1 C. sugar

Combine all ingredients and place in large container and freeze. To serve - fill glasses ⅔ full and add 7-Up to each glass to completely fill glass. Makes 24 cups of frozen slush.

SLUSH PUNCH

2 (6 oz. ea.) pkg. Jello
2 C. sugar
3 C. boiling water
1 (46 oz.) can pineapple juice
5 C. cold water
2 (32 oz.) bottles 7-Up

Add sugar and Jello to boiling water. Stir till dissolved. Add pineapple juice and cold water; freeze. Remove from freezer, about 2 hours before serving. Put into punch bowl and stir in 7-Up.

ROSY GLOW PUNCH

3 qt. cranberry cocktail juice
1 (12 oz.) can frozen lemonade
½ gallon raspberry sherbet
1 qt. gingerale (chilled)
Mint sprigs (optional)

Adding cranberry juice and lemonade, stir well and just before add scoops of raspberry sherbet. Slowly add gingerale. Makes 50 - 4 oz. servings.

HANKY PANKS

2 lbs. hamburger
1 lb. sausage
1 lb. Velveeta cheese
1 tsp. oregano
1 tsp. Worcestershire sauce
English muffins

Cook and drain hamburger and sausage. Mix and pour the cheese, oregano and sauce over meat. Spread on top of English muffins. Bake at 350° for 12 minutes.

PINK SQUIRRELS

2 oz. creme de almond
1½ oz. creme de cocoa (clear)
3 or 4 lg. ice cubes
Ice cream (vanilla)

Put in blender and mix until smooth.

GRAPE JUICE CRUSH

1 (24 oz.) bottle grape juice (chilled)
1 C. orange juice (chilled)
¼ C. lemon juice (chilled)
½ C. sugar
1 qt. gingerale (chilled) or club soda

Mix all ingredients, except gingerale. Stir in gingerale just before serving. Serve over ice. Makes 2 quarts.

CHICKEN SPREAD

1 C. chopped cooked chicken   3 T. lemon juice
1 C. chopped apple   3 T. mayonnaise
½ C. chopped celery

Mix all together and chill. Spread on salad greens, a meal in its self.

ORANGE JULIUS DRINK

6 oz. can frozen orange juice   1 tsp. real vanilla
6 oz. milk   6 ice cubes
6 oz. water

Blend all ingredients in blender. Makes four 6 oz. servings.

MINT COOLER

½ C. lemonade   2 scoops vanilla ice cream or
½ to 1 jigger green creme   rainbow sherbet
  de menthe   Fresh mint for garnish

In blender, place the lemonade, creme de menthe to taste, and ice cream or sherbet. Cover and blend till smooth. Pour into tall glasses, garnish with mint.

KAHLUA

2½ C. water
7 level T. Antigua coffee
4½ C. white sugar
1 tsp. vanilla
1/5 of Vodka

    Boil 2½ cup water. Remove ½ cup and dissolve Antigua coffee in it; set aside. In the remaining 2 cups water add sugar and boil 2 to 3 minutes on medium heat. Add the dissolved coffee to the syrup and cool. Then add 1 tsp. vanilla. Pour into an empty ½ gallon jug. Add 1/5 of the cheapest Vodka available. Turn gently. Can use in 1 week. Turn bottle each day. Use only Antigua Coffee (spice island). It is very delicious in a glass of milk with ice cubes.

LIME VODKA SLUSH

12 oz. can frozen orange juice
4 C. water
12 oz. can frozen lemonade
1 C. sugar
1 C. lime Vodka

    Combine all ingredients and serve over ice and 7-Up.

GREEN PUNCH

1 lg. can pineapple juice
1 pkg. lemon-lime Kool-Aid
2 C. sugar
Juice from 6 lemons

    In a large container, mix all ingredients. Add water to make 1½ gallons punch. For larger crowd, just double recipe.

CANDY & COOKIES

CHOCOLATE MARSHMALLOW COOKIES

2 sq. sweet chocolate
1 C. rich milk or ¾ C. evaporated milk &
   ¼ C. water
24 large marshmallows
1 tsp. vanilla

2 C. granulated sugar
1 T. butter
3 C. graham cracker crumbs
1 C. nuts

    Cook chocolate, milk and sugar to softball stage. Add butter and cool slightly. Add marshmallows (quartered), vanilla, graham cracker crumbs and nuts. Put in flat pan and cut in squares.

NO BAKE CHOCOLATE SQUARES

1½ C. white sugar
½ C. brown sugar
3 T. cocoa
¼ C. margarine

½ C. milk
3 C. oatmeal
½ C. peanut butter
1½ tsp. vanilla
Nuts (optional)

    Combine sugars and cocoa in large saucepan. Add margarine and milk. Bring to a boil, stirring well. Remove from heat. Add oatmeal, peanut butter, vanilla and nuts. Mix well. Pour into 9 x 9-inch pan. Let cool until firm. Cut into squares.

FUDGE

1 small can evaporated milk
1⅔ C. sugar
½ tsp. salt
1½ C. semi-sweet milk chocolate chips

1½ C. miniature marshmallows
1 tsp. vanilla
½ C. chopped nuts

Combine milk, sugar and salt in saucepan. Cook over low heat. Boil 3 minutes, stirring constantly. Add chips, marshmallows, vanilla and nuts. Stir well and pour into buttered pan. Makes 2 dozen pieces.

CHOP SUEY CANDY

Post Toasties (¾ box)
Rice Krispies (1 box)
1 C. salted peanuts.
1 C. coconut

2 C. white sugar
2 C. syrup (light or dark Karo)
2 C. cream
1 tsp. vanilla (optional)

Place cereals, nuts and coconut in large pan. Boil together the sugar, syrup and cream to a hard ball. Pour over ingredients in pan. Mix well and press down hard. When cool turn out on waxed paper and break into small pieces. To make half of this recipe, use 5 C. corn flakes, 3 C. Rice Krispies and ½ lb. peanuts. Divide remaining ingredients in half and proceed as given.

BREADS

HOCUS POCUS ROLLS

1 pkg. yeast
¾ C. warm water
1 egg
¼ C. shortening
¼ C. warm water
½ tsp. salt
½ C. sugar
1½ C. flour

Dissolve yeast in ¼ C. warm water. Add ¾ C. warm water, salt, egg, sugar, shortening and flour. Let rise; punch down and let rise again. Roll out and cut in 3½-inch circles. Put a large marshmallow, covered with butter, cinnamon and sugar in center of each. Draw up edges and seal. Butter and sugar top of each roll. Let rise. Bake until golden brown. Makes 24 rolls.

DROP DOUGHNUTS

2 T. butter
4 egg yolks
1 tsp. vanilla
3 C. flour
½ tsp. salt
¾ C. sugar
1 C. milk
½ tsp. lemon extract
3 tsp. baking powder
Dash nutmeg

Sift together dry ingredients and set aside. Beat egg yolks and add butter, sugar, milk, vanilla and lemon extract. Then add dry ingredients. Drop by teaspoons in hot fat, 375°. Drain on paper towels and roll in desired sugar.

GRAHAM JIM'S

1 C. white flour   1 C. graham flour
1 T. shortening   1 egg
1 C. milk   ¼ C. sugar
1 tsp. salt   2 tsp. baking powder

   Combine and bake in greased muffin pans at 375° for 20-25 minutes..

MUFFINS

1 banana   1 C. whole wheat flour
1 T. molasses   ¼ C. raisins
2 T. brown sugar   2 tsp. baking powder
1 egg   1 T. milk
¼ C. nutmeats

   Combine ingredients and bake 20 minutes at 350°.

DUMPLINGS

1 C. flour   1½ T. lard
1½ tsp. baking powder   ½ C. milk
Salt

   Mix together; roll or pat out ¼-inch thick. Cut in small squares. Drop in boiling broth and simmer 20 minutes.

BISCUITS

1 C. flour
¼ tsp. sugar   ½ T. Crisco
1 tsp. cream of tartar   ½ tsp. soda
¼ tsp. salt   ½ C. milk

    Make as you normally would for biscuits. Roll out or drop. Bake at 450° for 10-15 minutes.

HONEY BUTTER

1 stick oleo   ½ C. powdered sugar
1 C. honey   1½ tsp. cinnamon

    Beat together till thick. This is delicious on biscuits or hot rolls.

WAFFLES

2 C. all-purpose flour   3 egg yolks
½ tsp. baking soda   1¾ C. buttermilk
3 tsp. baking powder   ½ C. melted butter
¼ tsp. salt   3 egg whites, stiffly beaten
¼ C. sugar

    Combine flour, baking soda, salt, baking powder and sugar. Beat egg yolks with buttermilk. Add melted butter. Add liquid all at once into dry ingredients. Beat until smooth. Fold in egg whites. Bake to desired degree of doneness.

BRAN MUFFINS

1¼ C. sugar
1 C. plus 1 T. shortening
2 eggs
1 C. 100% Bran
1 C. boiling water
Raisins, optional

2 C. bran buds
2 C. buttermilk
3 C. flour
2½ tsp. soda
1 tsp. salt

Pour boiling water over 100% bran and let stand. Cream sugar, shortening and eggs. Add buttermilk and blend. Add bran buds and 100% bran and water; mix. Blend in flour, soda and salt. Bake at 400° for 12-15 minutes. Batter will keep in air tight container in the refrigerator for as long as 4 weeks.

DOUGHNUTS

6 eggs
2 C. sugar
1 tsp. salt
1 T. nutmeg
½ T. soda

2 T. baking powder
½ C. oil
1 tsp. vanilla
2 C. buttermilk
4 C. flour

Beat eggs; add sugar, salt and spice. Add oil, vanilla and buttermilk. Stir in 4-6 cups flour till dough is rather stiff. Turn out onto well-floured work area; work in enough more flour till dough is not sticky but soft. Pat to ¾ to 1-inch thickness. Cut with doughnut cutter and let rest about 10 minutes before frying in hot Crisco or oil. Add 2 T. vinegar to Crisco before heating to prevent doughnuts from being oily.

VEGGIES

EASY BAKED BEANS

3 or 4 strips bacon
1½ lb. can pork & beans
¾ C. brown sugar
¾ tsp. Worcestershire sauce
½ C. catsup
½ tsp. minced onions
Dash of hickory salt
Dash of garlic salt

Dice bacon and brown in skillet. Don't drain fat. Add remaining ingredients. Simmer 10 to 15 minutes. Remove from heat until ready to serve. Then heat quickly.

BROCCOLI AND RICE

1 C. chopped celery
1 T. chopped onion
1 C. cooked rice
2 pkgs. frozen broccoli
1 small jar Cheez Whiz
1 can cream of celery soup

Cook broccoli 6 minutes; set aside. Mix celery and onion, which have been browned in butter, rice, Cheez Whiz and soup. Put half of rice mixture in buttered casserole, layer of broccoli on top of rice, then add rest of rice mixture on top. Sprinkle with grated cheese. Bake at 350° for 30 minutes.

TANGY GREEN BEANS

2 strips of bacon
1 large onion
1 can tomato rice soup
1/8 tsp. basil
1 tsp. vinegar
1 qt. green beans

Brown bacon and onion in fat. Add remaining ingredients and heat thoroughly. Stir in ½ C. water.

SLICED CUCUMBERS

Sliced cucumbers   2 T. mayonnaise
Sliced onions   2 T. vinegar
Salt water   Lots of pepper

    Soak cucumbers and onions in salt water several hours; drain well. Combine mayonnaise, vinegar and pepper. Pour over cucumbers and onions, let set several hours in refrigerator.

CREAMED CUCUMBERS

¾ C. vinegar   Milk
Salt & pepper   1 carton sour cream
2 or 3 T. sugar   1 qt. salad dressing
Onion slices   Cucumber slices

    Mix vinegar, salt, pepper and sugar in a 2 cup measuring cup. Finish filling cup with milk, pouring slowly down side to curdle. Put in large mixing bowl, sour cream, stir up lumps. Add 1 quart salad dressing and let set 12 hours. Add cucumbers and onion slices. When cucumbers are gone dressing may be reused.

CHINESE STYLE FRIED RICE

Rice   1 egg (beaten)
3 T. butter   2-3 T. soy sauce
½ C. chopped onion   ⅓ C. water

    Cook 1 portion of rice. Cook egg in butter; add onion and rice, stirring over medium heat until rice and onion are lightly browned, about 5 minutes. Combine water and soy sauce; add to rice mixture, stir and eat.

CABBAGE CASSEROLE

1 medium sized head of cabbage	1 tsp. salt
1 tsp. sugar	Dash of pepper
2 T. flour	1 C. light cream

Shred cabbage and place in a greased casserole dish. Mix remaining ingredients and pour over cabbage. Cover with bacon strips. Cover dish until last few minutes of baking. Bake at 350° for about 40 minutes.

SCALLOPED CORN SUPREME

1 lb. can golden cream corn	¼ C. minced onion
1 C. milk	3 T. chopped pimento
1 well beaten egg	¾ tsp. salt
1 C. cracker crumbs	½ C. buttered cracker crumbs

Heat corn and milk. Gradually stir in egg. Add next 4 ingredients and a dash of pepper. Mix well and pour into greased 8-inch round baking dish. Sprinkle buttered crumbs over all. Bake at 350° for 20 minutes.

CABBAGE AND NOODLES

4 C. shredded cabbage	½ tsp. poppy seeds
1 small onion (thinly sliced)	2 C. cooked noodles
3 T. butter	½ tsp. salt
A little pepper	

IN a 2 quart casserole, combine all ingredients, except noodles. Cover and microwave at high for 5-6 minutes. Serve with sausage and beets.

BEAN CASSEROLE

1 T. mustard	1 can pork & beans
½ C. catsup	1 can butter beans (drained)
4 T. Karo syrup	1 can kidney beans (drained)
½ C. brown sugar	1 can lima beans (drained)
2 T. vinegar	1 can green beans (drained)
Salt	1 sm. bottle Worcestershire sauce
Onion	Bacon
Pepper	

Mix altogether. Good for crock pot or bean pot. May also add loose hamburger if desired.

SOUPS & SANDWICHES

BEAN CHOWDER

1 C. pinto beans
1 C. tomatoes
2 potatoes, diced
2 carrots, diced
½ lb. hamburger
4 T. bacon fryings
1 medium onion, diced

Soak beans overnight. Drain and add fresh water and cook until soft. Cook potatoes and carrots and add to beans, then add tomatoes. Fry hamburger and onion and add to the mixture. Salt and pepper to taste. Cook 15 minutes, stirring lightly. Serve with salad or pickles and corn meal muffins.

TUNA SANDWICHES

1 (7 oz.) can tuna
½ C. salad dressing
1 C. grated cheese
3 hard cooked eggs (chopped)
2 T. chopped pepper
2 T. chopped onion
2 T. chopped sweet pickles
6 hamburger buns

Combine all ingredients and mix well. Fill buns and wrap in aluminum foil. Heat in 250° oven until cheese melts - about 20 minutes.

SPECIAL SANDWICHES

Smoked ham (thinly sliced)
Chicken (thinly sliced)
Smoked beef (thinly sliced)
Swiss or Switzer cheese
3 C. flour
Dash of salt
1 tsp. baking powder
1 egg
Water
Powdered sugar

Make sandwiches by putting two slices of ham, chicken and beef between bread slices. Hold together with toothpick and then slice in half. Make a batter with remaining ingredients, except powdered sugar, and dip each sandwich half in batter. Deep fat fry each sandwich and drain. Sprinkle with powdered sugar.

PARTY SANDWICH FILLING

1 (8 oz.) soft cream cheese
¼ C. chopped onion
1 T. catsup
¾ tsp. salt
Dash of pepper
¾ C. chopped walnuts
3 T. chopped pimentos
3 hard cooked eggs
  (finely chopped)

Mix all ingredients thoroughly together. Lightly butter sandwich bread; spread filling between two slices of bread and cut into 4 triangles. Rye bread is also good.

HOT HAM AND CHEESE SANDWICHES

1 C. ham or minced ham (¼" cubes)
1 C. cheese (Cheddar or longhorn, 1¼" cubes)
½ C. chili sauce
½ C. chopped onions

Mix together and fill hot dog buns. Wrap each in foil. May be frozen until ready to heat. Heat till warm and cheese melts, 350° for 20-30 minutes. Allow extra time if frozen.

SALADS

FROZEN SALAD

1 large can crushed pineapple (not drained)
1 pkg. lime gelatin
1 pkg. small marshmallows
2 C. heavy cream
1 pkg. butter mints (crushed)

Mix Jello, crushed pineapple and marshmallows together, and soak overnight. No other liquid. Whip the heavy cream and fold crushed butter mints into it. Then fold all together and freeze. Cut into squares, or will make 21 paper baking cups.

FROZEN SALAD

9 oz. container Cool Whip
16 oz. crushed pineapple, drained
3 T. lemon juice
1 can Eagle Brand milk
½ tsp. lemon flavoring
Nut, chopped

Combine all ingredients. Freeze in paper cups in muffin tins. Yields 18.

FROZEN SALAD

1 big pkg. cream cheese
2 sm. cans crushed pineapples (drained)
½ C. mayonnaise
1 pkg. sm. marshmallows (could be colored)
1 C. nuts

Cream cheese and mayonnaise and mix with pineapple, marshmallows and nuts. Whip ½ pt. whipping cream and fold in above mixture. Put in freezer and freeze. Keeps well.

PRETTY PINK SALAD

1 13-oz. can crushed pineapple (don't drain)
1 3-oz. pkg. grape Jello
16 large marshmallows
1 8-oz. pkg. cream cheese (soft)
¼ C. milk
1 env. whipped topping, mixed

Heat first 3 ingredients until marshmallows are melted. Set aside to cool. In large bowl, beat cream cheese and milk till smooth. Fold in 1 envelope topping mix whipped according to directions. When gelatin mixture has cooled, combine the two mixtures and pour into attractive serving dish of your favorite mold. Refrigerate until set.

THREE FRUIT SALAD

2 pkg. strawberry gelatin
2 C. boiling water
1 can cranberry sauce jelly type
1 pkg. frozen strawberries
1 No. 303 can crushed pineapple

Dissolve gelatin in boiling water. Add cranberry sauce and mix well. Add strawberries and pineapple. Do not drain the fruit; let set. Best if allowed to set overnight.

"REAL McCOY" SALAD OR DESSERT

1 medium can crushed pineapple
1 3-oz. pkg. red Jello
1 small carton Cool Whip or
  1 box whipped topping (whipped)
1 C. pecans, chopped
1 small carton cottage cheese

Cook pineapple in its juice for 2 minutes. Add dry Jello. Cook 1 more minute; cool. Add remaining ingredients. Mix well and mold or gel in a bowl.

RED AND WHITE SALAD

1 pkg. lemon Jello
¾ C. boiling water
16 large marshmallows
1 pkg. whipped topping (prepared)
1 small pkg. cream cheese
½ C. crushed pineapple
½ C. Miracle Whip
1 pkg. strawberry Jello

Dissolve lemon Jello in water. Add marshmallows and stir until melted; let cool. Mix together: whipped topping, cream cheese, pineapple and Miracle Whip. Add to Jello-marshmallow mixture. Pour into 7 x 11-inch pan. Chill until set. Dissolve strawberry Jello according to package directions. When cool, pour over first mixture. Chill until set.

YUM-YUM SALAD

1 box lime Jello
1 C. hot water
1 C. nuts
1 small can pineapple
½ C. sugar
¾ C. grated cheese
1 C. whipping cream

Mix Jello, sugar and hot water. When begins to set, add rest of ingredients.

RASPBERRY SALAD

1 6-oz. pkg. raspberry Jello
1 C. water
1 can applesauce
2 pkg. frozen red raspberries

Dissolve Jello in 1 C. hot water and add fruit. Refrigerate until set.

RASPBERRY-APPLESAUCE SALAD

2 3-oz. pkg. raspberry Jello
2 C. hot water

2 C. applesauce
2 pkg. red raspberries (thawed)

TOPPING:
1 carton sour cream

8 oz. miniature marshmallows

Mix Jello, water and applesauce; cool. Add raspberries. Put in 9 x 13-inch pan. Mix sour cream and marshmallows. Let set out overnight. In the morning, whip and spread over Jello.

LAYERED STRAWBERRY SALAD

2 pkg. strawberry Jello
2 C. boiling water
2 10-oz. pkg. frozen strawberries

1 C. crushed pineapple
1 C. sour cream
1 C. walnuts or pecans
  (coarsely chopped)

Dissolve gelatin in boiling water. Add strawberries, stirring until dissolved. Fold in pineapple. Add nuts. Pour half of Jello mixture into a 8'' square dish. Chill until firm. Spread the sour cream over the chilled Jello. Very gently pour remaining Jello over top. Chill until firm. Cut into squares and serve on lettuce leaf.

PRETZEL SALAD

LAYER 1:
1 C. crushed pretzels   ⅓ stick margarine
1½ T. sugar
  Mix and press into 8" pan. Bake 10 minutes and cool.

LAYER 2:
2 3-oz. pkg. creamed cheese, softened   1 small carton Cool Whip or
½ C. sugar   Dream Whip
  Mix and spread on Layer 1.

LAYER 3:
1 pkg. strawberry Jello   1 pkg. frozen strawberries
  dissolved in 1 C. boiling water
  Add strawberries to Jello mixture. Cool and put on top and refrigerate.

TAPIOCA SALAD

½ C. minute tapioca   1 pkg. Dream Whip
2 C. water   1 can crushed pineapple
30 Circus peanuts
  Cook ½ C. minute tapioca with water until clear. Melt Circus peanuts in tapioca and cool. Add 1 pkg. Dream Whip (prepared) and crushed pineapple.

TAPIOCA SALAD

2 pkg. vanilla tapioca pudding
1 can crushed pineapple
1 can mandarin oranges or apricots, sliced
1 small box orange Jello
1 tub Cool Whip

Drain pineapple and apricots. Combine juice and enough water to make three cups. Bring to boil and add tapioca and return to boil, rolling. Remove from heat. Add orange Jello, cool till slightly congealed. Add the fruit and Cool Whip and **refrigerate**.

SALAD

3 eggs
Juice of 2 lemons or Real Lemon
¼ C. pineapple juice
3 T. sugar
1 lb. grapes, seeded & cut
2 cans crushed pineapple, drained
2 cans mandarin oranges, drained
½ pkg. small marshmallows
1 pt. cream

Cook first 4 ingredients until thicken, stirring all the time. Then whip the cream with the sauce and add fruit. Makes a large amount.

COLORED JELLO SALAD

1 pkg. orange Jello	1 C. pineapple juice
1 pkg. cherry Jello	¼ C. sugar
1 pkg. lime Jello	½ C. cold water
1 pkg. lemon Jello	2 C. Dream Whip
1½ C. vanilla wafers or	⅓ C. butter
graham cracker crumbs	

Add 1½ C. boiling water, separately to the following flavors of Jello: orange, cherry and lime. Let each set until firm and cut into small squares. Mix together pineapple juice and sugar. Heat until sugar is dissolved and add 1 pkg. lemon Jello and ½ C. cold water and stir. Thicken slightly and add Dream Whip. Stir the cut-up Jello into the lemon mixture. Mix the crushed wafers or graham cracker crumbs with butter. Pour crumb mixture into bottom of pan, reserving a few for the top of the dessert. Pour Jello mixture on top of crumbs and sprinkle reserved crumbs over the top.

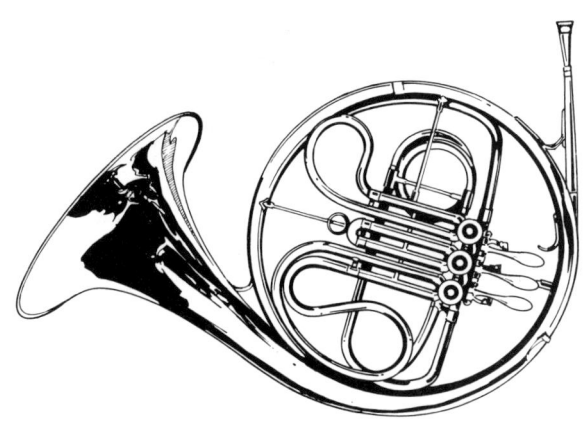

GOOD AND EASY LIME-LEMON SALAD

1 large box Jello or	1 C. hot water
2 regular size Jello	1 C. cold water
1 can lemon pudding	

Dissolve Jello in water, according to package instructions. Stir in pudding.

ICE CREAM JELLO SALAD

1 pkg. lemon Jello
1 C. boiling water
1 pt. vanilla ice cream
1 sm. can crushed pineapple, drain
1 C. grated Longhorn or American cheese

Dissolve Jello in boiling water. Add ice cream and stir until melted. Stir in pineapple and cheese. Refrigerate until set.

CHICKEN SALAD

1½ C. uncooked macaroni
1½ C. cooked chicken, diced
⅔ C. finely chopped celery
17 oz. can peas, drained
13¾-oz. can pineapple tidbits (drained)
¼ C. slivered almonds
2 T. diced pimento
1 C. Hellman's mayonnaise
2 T. lemon juice
1¼ tsp. seasoned salt
¼ tsp. pepper

Cook macaroni until done and drain. Combine macaroni, chicken, celery, peas, pineapple, almonds and pimento. Combine remaining ingredients in small bowl. Gently stir into chicken mixture. Cover and chill several hours.

CHICKEN SALAD

1 pkg. lemon Jello
1 tsp. vinegar
2 C. chicken broth
2 C. chopped chicken
½-2 C. chopped celery
2 pimentos (cut fine)
1 tsp. salt
1 C. heavy cream

Dissolve Jello with broth. When it sets, whip and add whipped cream together with rest of ingredients.

MAIN DISHES

EVERYDAY MEAT LOAF

2 beaten eggs	1 tsp. salt
¾ C. milk	½ tsp. ground sage
⅔ C. fine cracker crumbs	Dash pepper
2 T. grated onion	1½ lb. ground beef

TOPPING:

¼ C. catsup	1 tsp. dry mustard
2 T. brown sugar	¼ tsp. ground nutmeg

    Combine eggs, milk, bread crumbs, onion, salt, sage and pepper. Add beef and mix well. Pat mixture into 8½ x 4½ x 2½-inch loaf dish. Bake at 350° for 1 hour. Combine remaining ingredients. Spread over meat loaf. Bake 15 minutes longer. Makes 6 servings.

PARTY MEAT LOAF

2 lb. carrots	½ tsp. dried thyme leaves
1 C. finely chopped onion	1 T. salt
¼ C. butter	¼ tsp. pepper
1 tsp. salt	1½ lb. ground beef
Dash pepper	½ lb. ground pork (lean)
2 eggs	2 T. parsley
1 C. bread crumbs	Rest of onion
¼ C. milk	

    Make carrot filling with first 5 ingredients, reserving half of onion. Cook carrots until tender; mash. Makes 3 cups. Brown onion in butter until golden. Combine ½ of onion with carrots, salt and pepper. Mix meat loaf with rest of ingredients and roll out in rectangle. Spread meat evenly with carrot filling and roll up like jelly roll. Glaze with ½ C. catsup, 2 T. brown sugar and ¼ tsp. dry mustard. Bake uncovered 1 hour at 350°.

POTATO CHIP MEAT LOAF

1 lb. ground beef
½ lb. ground pork
2 slightly beaten eggs
⅔ C. crumbled potato chips
1 C. milk
½ tsp. salt
¼ C. chopped onion
1/8 tsp. pepper, Accent & basil
½ tsp. sage

Combine all ingredients and pack lightly into meat loaf pan. Bake at 350° for 1 hour. Serves four to six.

VEGETABLE MEATLOAF

1½ lb. ground lean beef
2 eggs
2 medium tomatoes, chopped
1 small onion, chopped
2 T. celery, chopped
2 T. parsley, chopped
1 small green chili (optional)
1 T. green pepper, chopped
½ C. non-fat dry milk
1 C. grated zucchini
½ C. grated carrot
½ tsp. sage
1¼ tsp. salt
Pepper
4 T. soy flour
1 C. whole wheat bread crumbs

Mix all of the above and bake at 350°.

SPICY POT ROAST

1 T. dry mustard
1 T. brown sugar
¼ tsp. pepper
1 tsp. poultry seasoning
1 tsp. salt or less
1 T. flour

Rub into meat and brown in hot pan in small amount of fat (browns nicely). Add ¼ C. hot water and 2 T. vinegar. Cook slowly on top of stove or in-oven. This mixture does several roasts and keeps ages.

TIM'S YUM YUM STEAK

BROWN IN OIL:
Chopped onion   Diced round steak
Chopped green pepper

ADD:
1 can mushroom soup   1½ C. minute rice
1 can cream of celery soup
   Cook for 45 minutes in skillet at low heat (add milk to keep moist if necessary.)

QUAIL AND PHEASANT FILETS

Quail or pheasant   Salt & pepper, to taste
¾ C. pancake flour   2 eggs
¼ C. yellow corn meal   2 T. milk
   Filet meat from bone. Cut into strips or can leave in large piece and pound it lightly. Combine the flour, corn meal and salt and pepper. Beat eggs and milk together. Dip filets in the egg mixture, then into flour mixture. Fry in skillet, moderate heat, until nicely browned on both sides.

HAM LOAF

1½ lb. pork roast, ground   1 C. bread crumbs
1½ lb. center ham, ground   ½ C. vinegar
2 eggs, well beaten
   Mix and wrap in cheese cloth molding loaves in desired size. Boil for 2 hours in water with the vinegar. Serve with sauce made of horseradish whipped into current jelly. Freezes well and may be reheated.

EGG CRUNCHY CASSEROLE

8 hard boiled eggs
1 can cream of celery soup or
    cream of chicken soup
½ tsp. onion flakes
Pepper to taste
2 T. milk
2 C. potato chips
Grated sharp cheese

    Slice and salt eggs. Layer in a buttered casserole dish. Mix together soup (undiluted), onion flakes, pepper and milk. Pour over eggs. Crush chips and mix with cheese. Sprinkle on top and bake at 350° for 25 to 35 minutes.

BARBECUE BEEF CUPS

¾ C. ground beef
½ C. barbecue sauce
1 tsp. instant minced onion
1 can refrigerated biscuits
¼ C. shredded American cheese

    Preheat oven to 400°. In a skillet, brown meat and pour off drippings. Add barbecue sauce and onion. Separate biscuits. Place each biscuit in an ungreased muffin cups, pressing dough up sides to edge of cup. Spoon meat mixture into cups. Bake 10 to 15 minutes or until golden brown. Sprinkle with cheese, return to oven until cheese is melted. Makes 10 beef cups.

EASY SPAGHETTI SAUCE

2 lb. ground beef
1 large onion, chopped
Garlic powder to taste
2 bay leaves
2 T. sweet basil
1 large can tomato paste
1 large can tomato sauce
2 cans water

    Brown ground beef and onion together. Add seasonings, then remaining ingredients. Simmer until thick.

CHINESE CASSEROLE

1 lb. lean ground beef	1½ C. warm water
2 medium chopped onions	½ C. uncooked rice
1 C. chopped celery	1/8 C. soy sauce
1 can cream of mushroom soup	¼ tsp. black pepper
1 can cream of chicken soup	1 can Chinese noodles

Brown meat and add onions, celery, soups and water. Stir in rice, soy sauce and pepper and put in 9 x 12-inch Pyrex dish. Bake in 350° oven for 30 minutes, cover with foil. Remove foil and continue baking another 30 minutes. Then spread can of noodles on top and bake 15 minutes. Serve with tossed salad and garlic bread.!

LASAGNE (Can Freeze)

2 T. oil	1 tsp. oregano
1 C minced onion	1 tsp. sugar
1½ lb. ground beef	1 tsp. basil
1 clove garlic, crushed	1 6-oz. can tomato paste
Salt	1 8-oz. can tomato sauce
16 oz. creamed style cottage cheese	2 beaten eggs
2 tsp. salt	½ tsp. pepper
2 T. parsley flakes	¾ C. Parmesan cheese
1 lb. lasagne noodles	1 lb. shredded mozzarella cheese

Brown ground beef, garlic, and onion in oil. Add oregano, sugar, basil, salt, tomato paste, tomato sauce and simmer 1 hour until thick. Combine cottage cheese, eggs, 2 tsp. salt, pepper, parsley flakes and Parmesan cheese. Cook lasagne noodles until tender. Place layer of noodles, layer of meat, layer of cheese mixture and shredded cheese in a baking dish (9 x 13-inch). Repeat until all ingredients are used. Bake at 375° for 35 to 45 minutes.

PIZZA CASSEROLE

2 lb. ground beef
1 medium onion
8 oz. noodles
  (cooked & drained)
Ragu sauce (18 oz.)
2 4-oz. cans mushrooms & liquid
Sliced stuffed olives
Mozzarella cheese

Brown ground beef and onion. Combine with remaining ingredients except cheese. Put in 9 x 13-inch pan. Top with grated cheese. Bake 20 minutes at 375°.

SPAGHETTI PIE

6 oz. spaghetti
2 T. butter
1/3 C. grated Parmesan cheese
2 beaten eggs
1 lb. hamburger
1/2 C. onion
1/4 C. green pepper
1 8-oz. can tomatoes (1 C.)
1 6-oz. can tomato paste
1 tsp. sugar
1 tsp. dried crushed oregano
1/2 tsp. garlic salt
1 C. (8 oz.) cottage cheese
1/2 C. mozzarella cheese

Cook spaghetti and drain. Stir in butter; add Parmesan cheese and eggs. Form crust in 10-inch pie plate. Cook beef, onion and pepper until brown; drain. Stir in undrained tomatoes, paste, sugar, oregano and garlic salt. Spread cottage cheese over crust. Fill with tomato and hamburger mixture. Bake uncovered for twenty minutes at 350°. Add mozzarella cheese and return to oven for ten minutes.

CHICKEN CASSEROLE

1 chicken (cut-up)
1½ C. rice (uncooked)
1 can celery soup
2 C. water
1 pkg. Lipton onion soup

Dilute celery soup with 2 C. of water and pour half of mixture in bottom of a large greased baking dish. Layer rice, chicken, onion soup and remainder of diluted celery soup. Bake 1½ hours at 350°. (Use large pan as rice swells.)

CHICKEN AND RICE

1½ C. uncooked rice
1 cut-up chicken
1 can chicken soup
1 can celery soup
1 can mushroom soup
¼ C. wine or apple juice
1 C. chopped cheese (optional)

Pour rice in buttered 9 x 13-inch pan. Place chicken pieces on rice. Pour soups and apple juice over all. If desired 1 C. chopped cheese may be added. Bake 1½ hours at 350°.

MACARONI AND CHEESE

1 pkg. Kraft dinner macaroni
6 C. boiling water
¼ C. margarine
¼ C. milk

Add macaroni to water; stir. Boil rapidly for 7 minutes - stirring occasionally or until desired tenderness is reached. Do not overcook; drain. Add margarine, milk and the cheese sauce. Mix well. (Save a little of cheese sauce, open envelope out flat and let cat lick off the paper.) Serve with boiled weiners.

SPANISH RICE

2 T. shortening
1 C. rice, uncooked
1 small onion, chopped
½ green pepper, diced
2 tsp. salt
2 tsp. chili powder
1 C. tomatoes
2 C. water

Heat the shortening and add the rice. Stir constantly until the rice is a light, golden brown. Add the other ingredients and cover tightly. Simmer slowly for about 20 minutes, until the rice is done and the liquid almost absorbed. Let stand about 10 minutes in the covered pan until the liquid is all absorbed into the rice. Put into covered casserole dish. Bake at 350° for 40 to 50 minutes, or until the rice is done.

BUTTERY SCALLOPED OYSTERS

1 pt. oysters
½ C. dry bread crumbs
½ C. melted butter
6 T. cream
1 C. cracker crumbs

Drain oysters. Combine liquid with cream. Mix bread crumbs and cracker crumbs. Add melted butter to crumbs and mix. Grease baking dish. Arrange in layers of crumbs then oysters. Dot with butter, season each layer. Pour liquid over all. Bake 20 minutes at 400° or until top is brown.

HAMBURGER CASSEROLE

2 lb. hamburger
Diced onions
Salt
1 box frozen peas
1 can cream of celery soup
1 box tater tots

Place hamburger in bottom of casserole dish. Cover with onions and salt. Layer on peas and pour soup over all. Top with tater tots. Bake at 350° for 2 hours.

DESSERTS

VANILLA ICE CREAM

3 C. scalded milk
2 T. cornstarch
½ C. milk
3 eggs, beaten

2 C. sugar
2 T. vanilla
2 to 3 C. cream
Milk to fill can

Scald the 3 C. of milk and then add cornstarch that was mixed with ½ C. of milk. Blend in the beaten eggs and cook until thick. Remove from heat and add sugar; beat until smooth. Stir in vanilla. Put in freezer can, add cream and milk to fill freezer can. Makes 1 gallon.

CHOCOLATE SAUCE

2 T. cornstarch
2 T. cocoa
¼ C. sugar

¾ C. white syrup
⅓ C. boiling water
1 T. butter

Combine cornstarch, cocoa and sugar; add syrup. Slowly add boiling water and boil for 5 minutes. Remove from heat and stir in butter; cool.

THREE IN ONE SHERBET

¾ C. orange juice
½ C. lemon juice
3 bananas (mashed)

3 C. sugar
3 C. water
3 egg whites (beaten)

Blend together juices, bananas, sugar and water; fold in beaten egg whites. Pour into freezer can and freeze.

"BEST HOMEMADE ICE CREAM"

4 eggs
1 pkg. Dream Whip (dry)
1 pkg. instant vanilla pudding (dry)
1½ to 1¾ C. sugar
½ gallon milk
Vanilla to taste

Beat eggs and sugar till creamy; add Dream Whip, pudding mix, milk and vanilla, stir until well blended. Pour into freezer can and freeze. Makes 1 gallon.

RHUBARB CRINKLE OR RHUBARB DELIGHT

1 C. flour
5 T. powdered sugar
½ C. oleo or butter

Mix and press into a 9 x 9-inch baking dish. Bake at 350° for 15 minutes, or until lightly browned.

2 eggs, beaten
1½ C. sugar
¼ C. flour
¾ tsp. salt
2 C. rhubarb

Mix eggs, sugar, flour, salt and rhubarb together. Spoon over baked crust. Bake at 350° for 35 minutes.

HOMEMADE PEACH ICE CREAM

2 pkg. (3 oz.) peach Jello
2 C. boiling water
3 C. sugar
4 eggs (well beaten)
2 C. heavy cream
4 C. milk
2 tsp. vanilla
2 sm. cans peaches (cut in pieces)

Dissolve Jello in boiling water; let cool. Add sugar, eggs, cream, milk and vanilla. Stir until well blended. May use a mixer. Stir in peaches. Pour into freezer can and freeze. Makes 1 gallon.

IMPROVE-
MENT OF
MUSCLE
TONE

APPETIZERS & BEVERAGES

HOT COCOA MEXICANA

½ C. Hershey's cocoa
1 tsp. ground cinnamon
¼ tsp. ea. nutmeg & allspice
1/8 tsp. salt
½ C. hot tap water

4 C. milk
2 beaten eggs
½ C. Kahlua
Whipped cream
Nutmeg

In a large saucepan, combine cocoa, cinnamon, nutmeg, allspice, and salt. Blend in water and bring to a boil over medium heat, stirring constantly. Continue stirring for 2 minutes. Add milk and heat thoroughly, but do not boil again. Ladle out ½ cup of this and blend into beaten eggs. Pour into saucepan. Stir and heat again, but do not boil. Stir in Kahlua, pour into mugs, add whipped cream and a dash of nutmeg.

FROZEN DACQUARI

28 ozs. 7-Up
28 oz. of club soda
16 oz. Squirt

1/5 of Rum
4 cans (6 oz. ea.) lemonade
3 cans (6 oz. ea.) limeade

Put all ingredients in a punch bowl or container and put in freezer.

KAHLUA LIQUOR

4 C. sugar
½ C. instant coffee
3 C. water

Dash of salt
2½ C. Vodka
3 T. vanilla

Combine sugar, coffee and water; bring to a boil until sugar dissolves. Simmer for about 1 hour. Remove from flame. Add vanilla and Vodka.

SPINACH BALLS

2 (10 oz. ea.) pkgs. frozen chopped spinach
3 C. herb seasoned stuffing mix
1 lg. onion (finely minced)
6 eggs (well beaten)
¾ C. melted butter or margarine

½ C. grated Parmesan cheese
1 T. pepper
1½ tsp. garlic salt
½ tsp. thyme

Cook spinach, according to package directions, drain well and squeeze to remove excess moisture. Combine spinach and remaining ingredients, mixing well. Shape ¾" balls for appetizers or in larger balls for a vegetable dish. Bake at 325° on lightly greased cookie sheet 15-20 minutes. Cook the larger balls 5 minutes longer. Balls may be frozen before baking until firm on a cookie sheet. Then store frozen balls in a plastic bag.

HOT CHOCOLATE MIX

1 lb. powdered sugar
20 qt. powdered milk

1 lb. & 1 sm. can Quick
1 lg. Coffee Mate

Mix all together. Store in tightly covered containers (I store it in the freezer.) Place 2 T. mix in a cup. Add hot water and stir.

DRY HOT CHOCOLATE MIX

1 (8 qt.) pkg. non-fat dry milk powder
1 (16 oz.) can sweetened cocoa mix
1 lb. sifted powdered sugar
1 (6 oz.) jar powdered non-dairy creamer

    Mix ingredients together well. Makes 15 cups of mix. Stores well. To mix drink: Mix ¼ cup mix with 1 cup boiling water.

VEGETABLE DIP

1 C. sour cream
1 C. mayonnaise
1 T. parsley flakes
1 T. dill weed
1 T. onion flakes
1 T. beau monde spice island

    Mix all ingredients well and refrigerate overnight or longer. May add salt, pepper and chives to taste.

VEGETABLE DIP

1 carton sour cream
1 C. mayonnaise
1½ tsp. green onions & tops (chopped fine)
1½ tsp. parsley flakes
1½ tsp. dill weed
1½ tsp. beau monde seasoning

    Mix well and chill 3 hours before serving.

DIP FOR RAW VEGETABLES

1 C. mayonnaise
2 T. grated onion
1 tsp. curry powder
1 tsp. garlic powder

Blend well in blender or food processor and refrigerate until ready to use.

SHRIMP MOLD

8 oz. pkg. cream cheese
4 oz. shrimp
2 T mayonnaise
½ tsp. Accent
1 clove garlic (minced)
¼ C. grated onion
Hot sauce, to taste

Mix all together; chill and mold. Serve as spread on cracker.

SPINACH BALLS

2 pkgs. spinach (cooked, drained & chopped)
2 C. herb bread stuffing mix
2 lbs. onion (minced)
6 lg. eggs (beaten)
¼ C. melted butter
½ C. Parmesan cheese
½ tsp. thyme
1 big T. garlic salt
1 tsp. pepper

Drain spinach well. Mix all. Form into small balls. Bake for 20 minutes at 350°.

CANDY & COOKIES

THREE LAYER BARS

½ C. butter
¼ C. sugar
⅓ C. cocoa
1 tsp. vanilla
1 egg, beaten
½ C. butter

1½ T. milk
2 T. vanilla instant pudding mix
2 C. powdered sugar
6 oz. semi-sweet chocolate chips
1 T. butter or more

Place butter (½ C.), ¼ C. sugar, cocoa and vanilla in top of double boiler and cook until blended. Add egg, slowly and cook 5 minutes, stirring constantly. Mix and press into 9 x 9 x 2-inch pan. Let this stand 15 minutes, then put on second layer.

Second Layer: Cream ½ C. butter, milk and pudding mix (dry). Mix well and add 2 C. powdered sugar. Let stand 15 minutes or until firm, then put on the last layer.

Third Layer: Melt chocolate chips and 1 T. butter. Spread over all and cool.

DIVINITY CANDY

3 C. sugar
¾ C. white syrup
2 egg whites

½ C. water
Vanilla
Nuts (optional)

Cook sugar, water and syrup over low heat. Stir till sugar is dissolved. Cover till crystals are dissolved. Boil to 248°, set off while beating egg whites. Pour syrup slowly over egg whites while beating. Add vanilla, continue beating till a spoon will stand up in mixture. Add nuts, if desired. Drop on waxed paper by spoonfuls. Store in a cool dry place.

OLD FASIONED CUT COOKIES

1 C. brown sugar	2 C. flour
½ C. butter	1 tsp. soda
1½ C. raisins	1 tsp. baking powder
1 C. hot water	1 tsp. cinnamon
Dash salt	Nuts (optional)
2 T. hot water	

Put brown sugar, butter, raisins, hot water and salt in a pan, bring to a boil and boil for 3 minutes. Let cool. Add the 2 T. hot water, flour, soda, baking powder, cinnamon and nuts. Beat together and spread on cookie sheet or jelly roll pan. Bake at 350° for about 12-15 minutes. Frost hot and cut in squares.

CREAM CHEESE MINTS

1 lb. powdered sugar	Peppermint oil
3 oz. pkg. cream cheese	Food coloring
1 T. white Karo syrup	

With cheese at room temperature, mix it with syrup until smooth. Add coloring and a few drops of peppermint oil. Stir in powdered sugar a little at a time, then knead. (May not be able to work the full pound of sugar in.) Make into little balls and press down, or use a mint mold.

WEDDING MINTS

1 lb. powdered sugar	Drop of wintergreen oil or 1 t. mint
1 3-oz. pkg. cream cheese	Food coloring

Method 1: Mix, roll out ¼-inch thick, cut with small medicine bottle. Tap with meat cleaver to make design. Approximately 70-75 small mints.

Method 2: Form into balls and roll in sugar. Press into mold. Remove from mold. Freeze or refrigerate until 1 hour before using.

BREADS

CINNAMON ROLLS

1 stick oleo
2 T. cinnamon
1 C. sugar
2 tubes of biscuits

TOPPING:
1 C. brown sugar
¼ C. milk
1 T. oleo

Melt oleo in saucepan. Mix cinnamon and sugar together. Dip each biscuit in oleo and then dip in cinnamon and sugar. Arrange in 9 x 13-inch pan. Mix topping in saucepan and heat till smooth. Pour over biscuits and bake at 400° for 25-30 minutes. (For a change I add raisins and nuts.)

OATMEAL MUFFINS

1 C. quick oatmeal
1 C. flour
3 tsp. baking powder
1 egg
1 C. milk
⅓ C. sugar
½ tsp. salt
¼ C. salad oil

Combine oatmeal and milk. Let stand 15 minutes. Sift flour, sugar, baking powder and salt into bowl. Combine egg, oil and oatmeal mixture. Add all at once to sifted dry ingredients, stirring just to moisten. Fill greased muffin pans ⅔ full. Bake at 400° for 20-25 minutes. Makes about 1 dozen.

CORN BREAD

1 C. corn meal
1 C. sifted flour
3 tsp. baking powder
1 tsp. salt
2 T. sugar
1 egg, beaten
1 C. milk
½ C. cooking oil

Sift and mix all dry ingredients together. Add egg, milk and oil; mix well. Pour into well greased 9 x 9 x 2-inch pan. Bake at 400° for about 30 minutes.

PANCAKE MIX

12 C. flour	2 T. salt
¾ C. baking powder	¾ C. sugar
4 C. dry milk	

Mix and store in air-tight container. When ready to use, for each 1½ cups pancake mix (to serve 6 persons) use:

1 egg, beaten	2 T. melted shortening (or oil)
1 C. water	

Mix well and fry on a hot griddle.

NOODLES

1 egg	1 T. cream
1 C. flour	Pinch of salt

Mix well and roll thin. Then cut into strips, dry 1 hour.

RIVELS

1 C. flour	½ tsp. salt
1 egg	Hot soup or broth

Put flour and salt in a bowl. Make a well in the middle. Add beaten egg and stir with a fork or fingers until the egg has taken up all the flour and the mixture becomes crumbly, like coarse grains of rice. If a large egg is used you may need a little more flour. Rub the rivels between the fingers as they are dropped into hot boiling chicken broth, potato soup, bean soup or vegetable stew. Cook, stirring occasionally for about 10 minutes. This is an old-fashioned recipe.

HUSH PUPPIES

1 egg, beaten
1 C. corn meal
2 tsp. baking powder
1 onion

1 T. flour
½ tsp. salt
¼ C. milk

    Mix dry ingredients together. Add finely chopped onion, then milk and beaten egg. Press in finger shapes, pones, or balls or drop from spoon into pan or kettle in which fish has been fried. Fry to golden brown. Drain on paper. Note: Hush puppies is a Southern dish cooked at all fish fries and hunting trips. At first they were made to feed the hungry howling hounds or hunting dogs to keep them quiet; hence "hush puppies". Later they were carefully made and eaten by the entire party. This old colonial custom has been handed down to the present day.

APPLE-NUT-CHEESE BISCUITS

⅓ C. sugar
½ tsp. cinnamon
1 small apple, chopped
⅓ C. cold water
¼ C. margarine or butter

⅓ C. chopped walnuts
1¾ C. packaged biscuit mix
¾ C. shredded sharp Cheddar cheese

    Stir together sugar, nuts and cinnamon; set aside. Stir together biscuit mix, cheese and apple. Make a well in center of mixture, stirring just until moistened. Form into a ball. Flatten out on floured surface. Divide into 18 pieces, shape each into a ball. Roll in melted butter; then in sugar mixture. Arrange in greased 9-inch round pan. Bake at 400° for 25-30 minutes.

LONG JOHN'S

2 pkg. dry yeast
1 C. warm water
¾ C. sugar
3 tsp. salt

1 tsp. sugar
2 C. milk
¾ C. lard
3 eggs

FROSTING:
1 box powdered sugar
1 T. Crisco
Milk

1 T. butter
1 T. vanilla

Dissolve yeast in warm water with 1 tsp. sugar. Heat milk to boiling point and add sugar, lard and salt; cool. Beat eggs, or for lighter dough use 6 egg yolks with ¾ cup mashed potatoes. Add to yeast mixture. Then add as much flour as can be easily stirred with spoon. Let stand 15 minutes to lighten. Add just enough flour to hand (no more). Let rise until light. Punch down and let rise again. Roll out ½-inch thick and cut in strips about 1½ to 2¾-inches. Put on greased or floured cookie sheet. Let rise till double in size, about 1 hour. Fry in hot fat. Makes 5 dozen. Combine ingredients to make frosting, using enough milk to make spread and roll in brown sugar. These freeze very well.

SWEET ROLLS

2 C. milk
2 tsp. salt
2 eggs
7-7½ C. flour

½ C. sugar
2 pkg. yeast
½ C. shortening

Scald milk and cool to lukewarm. Add sugar and salt. Stir in yeast, eggs, shortening and flour in two additions, beating well. Keep dough as soft as possible, almost sticky - just so you are able to handle it. Let rise once, punch down and let rise again. Then shape into rolls, or roll out and cut. Let rise until light. Bake in 400° oven for about 15 minutes.

VEGGIES

ASPARAGUS CASSEROLES

1 can cream of chicken soup
¼ C. milk
3 hard-cooked eggs
1 tsp. onion flakes
1 C. cubed American cheese
1 pkg. frozen cut asparagus
1 C. sliced almonds
½ C. bread crumbs
2 T. butter

    Combine milk and soup. Cut eggs in 1/8-inch slices and stir in eggs, cheese and asparagus (which has been cooked until tender). Turn mixture into buttered casserole. Cover top with almonds, then crumbs. Dot with butter. Bake at 350° for 30 to 40 minutes until bubbly and slightly brown.

ASPARAGUS WITH HOLLANDAISE SAUCE

4 egg yolks
Juice of 1 lemon
4 T. boiling water
1 stick butter
1½ to 2 lbs. asparagus (cooked)

    Put the yolks in a small glass bowl and beat with lemon juice and boiling water. Heat the butter in a saucepan over high heat, as soon as it is melted, remove from heat and pour the yolk mixture into the saucepan all at once. Stir continuously until sauce is thick and well blended. Pour over hot asparagus or serve on the side.

BARBEQUED GREEN BEANS

6 slices bacon
1 medium onion, chopped
1 can tomato soup or sauce
2 T. sugar
1 tsp. dry mustard
Salt & pepper
1 can mushrooms (drained)
2 cans whole green beans (drained)

Cut bacon in small pieces and brown in heavy pan. Add onions and brown, stirring often. Add tomato soup or sauce, sugar, dry mustard and seasonings. Fold in mushrooms and green beans. Simmer slowly for 30 minutes.

BEANS SUPREME

1 can green beans
2 eggs
1½ C. liquid (milk & bean liquid)
4 slices bread, cubed
1 C. grated cheese
Salt & pepper, to taste

Combine beaten eggs, milk, salt and pepper. Alternate layers of beans, bread and cheese in a buttered casserole. Add milk mixture and bake 45 minutes in a moderate oven.

BAKED BEANS

½ C. chopped onion
¼ C. molasses
1 T. mustard
6 frankfurters
½ tsp. Worcestershire sauce
½ C. catsup
2 #2 cans pork (5 C.) pork & beans

Mix together first six ingredients. Place in quart casserole and bake in slow oven (300°) for 1½ hours. Lay franks on beans and bake another 30 minutes and serve.

BEAN BAKE

8 slices bacon
1 C. vinegar
1 C. brown sugar
¼ tsp. dry mustard
Garlic (if you like)
1 large onion, chopped

1 large can each of:
large butter beans
small green lima
green beans
red kidney beans
Morton house baked beans
(all drained)

Fry bacon, cool and crumble. Discard most of the grease. To about 1 T. of grease, add vinegar, sugar, mustard and onion. Simmer about 20 minutes. Pour over the beans in a large casserole or bean pot with bacon. Bake at 350° for 1 hour. Strips of cheese may be put on top for the last 10 minutes.

CALICO BEANS

½ lb. bacon
½ lb. ground beef
½ C. chopped onion
½ C. catsup
1 tsp. salt
½ to ¾ C. brown sugar

1 T. mustard
3 T. vinegar
1 No. 2 can lima beans (or can use butter beans)
1 No. 2 can red beans
1 No. 2 can pork & beans

Cook bacon until crisp, drain and crumble. Cook beef and drain. Add all seasonings. Drain off all the bean liquids. Add everything together in a big baking pan. Stir gently. Sprinkle bacon on top. Bake at 350° for 60 minutes.

BROCCOLI WITH CASHEWS (Serves 6)

1 large bunch fresh broccoli or
  2 10-oz. pkg. frozen
2 T. minced onion
2 T. butter
1 C. sour cream
2 tsp. sugar
1 tsp. vinegar
½ tsp. poppyseeds
¼ tsp. salt
½ tsp. paprika
1 C. roasted cashews

    Cook broccoli in water until crisp. Saute onion in butter. Stir in sour cream and remaining ingredients, except cashews. Layer broccoli in a buttered 1½ quart baking dish and cover with sauce. Sprinkle with cashews and bake uncovered at 325° for 25 minutes.

BROCCOLI CASSEROLE

½ C. celery (chopped)
1 onion
3 T. butter
1 pkg. chopped broccoli
1 can cream of chicken soup
2 C. rice (cooked)
1 8-oz. jar Cheez Whiz

    Saute celery, onion and butter. Add broccoli. Stir until it comes apart. Add chicken soup, rice and Cheez Whiz. Mix together well. Place in baking dish and bake 30 minutes at 350°.

BROCCOLI CASSEROLE

2 10-oz. pkg. broccoli
Crushed Ritz crackers
Cheese slices
1 stick oleo

    Cook broccoli until tender. Put into 8 x 8-inch greased pan. Top with cheese slices. Put crushed Ritz crackers on top of cheese and top with oleo, cut into chunks. Bake at 350° for 30 minutes.

SOUPS & SANDWICHES

HAM AND CORN CHOWDER

3 slices bacon
4 medium potatoes (diced)
2 medium onions (chopped)
1 C. celery (diced)
2 (13 oz. ea.) cans chicken broth

1½ C. corn (drained)
2 T. flour
2 C. ham (diced)
3 C. milk
Salt & pepper, to taste

Fry bacon until crisp. Remove and set aside. Saute onion and celery in bacon drippings. Sprinkle with flour. Stir in chicken broth and potatoes. Simmer until potatoes are tender. Add ham, corn and milk. Heat thoroughly but do not boil. Season to taste.

5 HOUR STEW

2 lbs. stew beef (bite size)
1 C. celery (chopped)
2 potatoes (cubed)
6 carrots (cut in pieces)
1 slice bread (cubed)

2 (8 oz. ea.) cans tomato sauce
1 C. water
1½ tsp. salt
½ tsp. pepper
½ onion (cut-up)

Combine all ingredients in casserole. Cover and bake at 250° for 5 hours. Easy and good. Serves 6.

BROILED SANDWICHES

1 can Spam (ground)
¼ C. catsup
1 T. onion (minced)

2 T. sugar
2 T. vinegar

Broil on open buns until brown.

TOMATO NOODLE SOUP

1½ lbs. stewing beef
1 onion (diced)
Salt & pepper, to taste
1 can or pt. tomatoes

1 small can V-8 juice
2 or 3 stalks celery
½ tsp. chili powder
½ pkg. noodles

Brown meat and onion, then add salt and pepper. Mash tomatoes and add to above. Add juice, celery and chili powder. Cook until tender. Add cooked noodles.

SUBMARINE SANDWICH

On buns or slices of French bread, place thin slices of beef. Add a layer of shredded mozzarella cheese and a layer of lettuce. Top with Italian dressing. Wrap in aluminum foil and place in 350° oven until heated through. Serve warm.

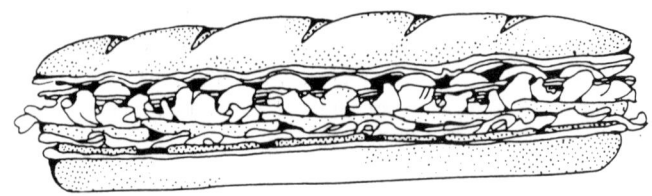

CHEESE AND BEER SOUP

½ C. butter
1 C. flour
4 C. chicken broth
1½ C. Half & Half
16 oz. jar Cheez Whiz

6 ozs. beer
1 T. Worcestershire sauce
½ tsp. yellow food coloring
¼ C. dried chives

In a heavy pan melt butter. Mix in flour until blended. Heat over low burner for about 5 minutes, stirring occasionally. Add broth, cream and Cheez Whiz. Mix until all cheese is melted and soup is smooth. Add beer and Worcestershire sauce. Mix in coloring and chives. Simmer for about 10 to 15 minutes. Stir constantly. Serve with a bowl of popcorn. This is a must! Sprinkle a few pieces of popcorn into soup bowl at a time so they remain crunchy.

BEEF STEW

4 lbs. stew meat
3 or 4 T. flour
2 cans beef consomme
1 T. dried parsley
2 bay leaves

2 C. red wine - burgundy
6 or 8 carrots
1 small can onions
1 large can mushrooms

Brown meat in Dutch oven; add flour and brown some more. Add little fat if it sticks too much. Add consomme, parsley, bay leaves, wine and then water to cover water. Simmer 2 hours. Add more water if it gets too thick or too low. Add carrots and salt to taste and simmer another two hours, or until carrots are done, or stew starts to thicken. Add onions and mushrooms. Let simmer 10-15 minutes. Serve with green salad and bread.

SALADS

APPLE SALAD

1 dozen apples
1 can pineapple
1 lb. grapes

1 C. nutmeats
1 dozen marshmallows
Juice of 1 lemon

DRESSING:
Juice of pineapple
3 eggs
1 C. sugar

2 T. flour
2 T. butter

Heat pineapple juice and stir in beaten eggs, flour and sugar. Cook till thick. Stir in ½ pt. whipped cream, just before adding to fruit mixture.

APRICOT SALAD

2 pkg. orange Jello
1 C. apricots
1 C. miniature marshmallows

2 C. boiling water
1 can crushed pineapple

TOPPING:
1 C. juice (apricot & pineapple)
2 T. flour
2 T. butter
½ C. sugar

1 egg, beaten
1 C. whipped topping
Grated cheese

Mix first five ingredients and let set until firm in 9 x 13-inch glass baking dish. Cook juice, sugar, flour and egg until thick. Add butter and cool. Add 1 C. whipped topping. Frost the first mixture. Top with grated cheese.

BLUEBERRY SALAD

FIRST LAYER:
1 pkg. raspberry Jello   2 C. boiling water
   Pour into 8 x 12-inch pan and chill until firm.

SECOND LAYER:
1 env. Knox gelatin   1 C. sugar
1 C. half & half or canned milk   8 oz. pkg. cream cheese, softened
1 tsp. vanilla   ½ C. nuts
½ C. cold water
   Soften gelatin in cold water. Heat milk and sugar until hot, but do not boil. Stir in softened gelatin. Add vanilla and cream cheese; blend until smooth. Stir in nuts. Pour on top of first layer. Chill until firm.

THIRD LAYER:
1 pkg. raspberry Jello   1 C. hot water
1 can blueberries (No. 303)
   Dissolve Jello in hot water and stir. Add blueberries, juice and all. Pour over the other layers and let set. (Be sure the second and third layer ingredients are not too hot when poured over the preceding layers.)

BLUEBERRY SALAD

1 6-oz. box raspberry Jello   1 sm. can crushed pineapple, drain
2 C. hot water   2 env. Dream Whip
1 lb. can blueberries, undrained   1 C. chopped pecans
   Dissolve Jello in hot water; add blueberries with syrup and pineapple. Chill until partially set. Prepare Dream Whip. Add Dream Whip and nuts to Jello mixture. Refrigerate until completely set. Fills a 9 x 13-inch pan.

APRICOT SALAD

1 can apricot pie filling
1 can chunk pineapple, drained
1 small jar maraschino cherries (drained & halved)
1½ C. small marshmallows
4 bananas

Stir together and chill. At last minute add 4 bananas. Serve on lettuce leaf.

ETHEL CUNNINGHAM'S CRANBERRY SALAD

4 C. cranberries
2 oranges
1½ C. sugar
½ C. pecans

Remove peel from ¾ of orange. Quarter and remove seeds. Put oranges and sugar into blender on chop speed. Empty into bowl. Chop cranberries at same speed. Mix with oranges and chopped nuts and chill.

DELIGHTFUL BLUEBERRY SALAD

2 3-oz. pkg. raspberry Jello
3 C. hot water
1 can blueberry pie filling
1 pkg. cream cheese
1 pkg. Dream Whip

Dissolve Jello and cool. Add pie filling. Chill until firm. Soften and whip cream cheese. Prepare package of Dream Whip. Mix cream cheese with Dream Whip. Spread on Jello mixture.

CHERRY SALAD SUPREME

1 3-oz. box raspberry Jello
1 can cherry pie filling
1 3-oz. box lemon Jello
⅓ C. salad dressing
1 3-oz. pkg. cream cheese
1 C. crushed pineapple
2 C. boiling water
1 pkg. Dream Whip
1 C. small marshmallows
1 T. chopped nuts

Dissolve raspberry Jello in 1 C. boiling water. Stir in pie filling. Put mixture into salad bowl and chill until partially set. Dissolve lemon Jello in 1 C. boiling water. Beat together salad dressing and cream cheese and add gradually to cooled lemon Jello. Stir in undrained pineapple. Whip Dream Whip according to package directions. Fold into lemon mixture. Add marshmallows. Spread lemon mixture on top of raspberry mixture. Sprinkle nuts on top. Chill until set. (Cool Whip may be spread on top before nuts are added.)

PURPLE MOLD

1 can dark sweet cherries (pitted)
1 13-oz. can pineapple chunks
1 8-oz. pkg. cream cheese
¼ C. pineapple juice
½ C. cherry juice
1 env. Dream Whip
1 C. small marshmallows

Soften cream cheese and beat with juices until smooth. Add well drained fruit and fold in prepared Dream Whip and marshmallows. Put in lightly oiled mold. Chill in refrigerator.

CRANBERRY SALAD

1 qt. cranberries
1½ C. sugar
1 can crushed pineapple (save juice)

2 pkg. wild strawberry Jello
2 C. boiling water

TOPPING:
1 C. pineapple juice
2 T. butter
2 T. flour

½ C. sugar
1 egg, beaten

Grind cranberries in blender with small amount of water, ½ C. at a time. Mix ground cranberries, sugar and pineapple and let stand for 2 hours. Dissolve Jello in hot water, then let cool. When cool, mix cranberries and Jello; let set. Cook topping ingredients till thick. Let cool. Mix with quart size Cool Whip and spread on Jello.

CHRISTMAS JELLO

1 pkg. lime Jello
1 pkg. lemon Jello
15 marshmallows
½ C. sugar

1 C. whipped cream
1 pkg. cream cheese
1 can crushed pineapple
1 pkg. cherry Jello

Dissolve lime Jello and set in 9 x 9-inch dish. Dissolve lemon Jello in ½ C. hot water. Mix in marshmallows while Jello is hot. Add ½ C. sugar. Cool til beginning to set. Add whipped cream, pineapple and cream cheese. Pour over first Jello and set. Dissolve the cherry Jello and cool til syrup like and pour over top; set.

CRANBERRY SALAD

½ lb. cranberries
2 oranges, diced
2 pkg. red Jello
2 C. sugar
2 C. diced apples
2 stalks celery, chopped
Nutmeats
Pineapple (optional)

    Mix cranberries and oranges. Cover with sugar and refrigerate for 4 hours. Dissolve Jello in 3 C. hot water. Cool and add cranberry mixture. Add apples, celery and nutmeats. Add pineapple if desired.

HEAVENLY CRANBERRY SALAD

1 pkg. ground cranberries
1 C. sugar
1 pkg. Dream Whip (whipped)
1 No. 303 can crushed pineapple
1 C. small marshmallows
½ C. nuts

    Mix cranberries, pineapple and sugar thoroughly and let stand overnight. Add remaining ingredients, mix and refrigerate.

CRANBERRY-RASPBERRY SALAD

2-3 oz. pkg. cherry Jello
1½ C. hot water
1 16-oz. can whole cranberry sauce
1 8-oz. can crushed pineapple
2-3 oz. pkg. raspberry Jello
1 pt. sour cream
1½ C. hot water
2 10-oz. pkg. frozen raspberries

    Dissolve cherry Jello in hot water. Add cranberry sauce and drained pineapple. Pour into 13 x 9 x 2-inch dish and let set. When set, spread sour cream over this. Mix raspberry Jello and water. Add frozen berries and let gel a little. Pour this over sour cream layer. Serves 12

GOLDEN FLECK SALAD

3 oz. pkg. orange Jello
3 oz. pkg. cream cheese
   (softened & broken to bits)
1 C. small marshmallows
1 tsp. lemon flavoring

Pour 1¾ C. boiling water over above ingredients and stir until dissolved; cool and add:

1 C. grated carrots
½ C. chopped pecans
1 C. crushed pineapple (drained)
1 C. whipped topping

Pour into 8 x 8-inch dish and refrigerate. (Pineapple juice may be heated for part of the liquid (water) required.)

PEAR SALAD

1 3-oz. pkg. lime Jello
1 C. pear juice
2 3-oz. pkg. cream cheese (room temp)
#1 can pears (drained)
½ tsp. lemon flavoring
1 C. cream (whipped) or 2 oz. pkg. whipped topping (prepared)
½ C. quartered maraschino cherries
⅓ C. chopped pecans

Dissolve Jello in the boiling pear juice. Add lemon flavoring and beat in the cream cheese. Add pears which have been drained and crushed. Chill until mixture is syrupy. Then fold in the whipped cream (or topping mix), cherries and nuts. Pour into 9-inch square pan. Chill until firm.

FROZEN PEACH SALAD

1 can peach pie filling
1 small can crushed pineapple (drained)
1 can Eagle Brand milk
¼ C. lemon juice
½ tsp. almond flavoring
1 small carton Cool Whip

   Mix ingredients together and freeze.

ACINI DE PEPE

1 pkg. spaghetti (rings)	1 bag small marshmallows
2 cans chunk pineapple	1¾ C. pineapple juice
(drained & save juice)	1 C. sugar
2 cans mandarin oranges (drained)	1 tsp. salt
1 large carton Cool Whip	2 T. flour
Handful of coconut	2 eggs, beaten

    Mix together pineapple juice, sugar, salt and flour. Bring to a boil. Add part of sauce to beaten eggs, then gradually blend egg mixture in with rest of sauce. Cook 2 to 3 minutes longer till thick and cool. Add to cooked and cooled spaghetti. Refrigerate overnight. Add pineapple, oranges, Cool Whip, coconut and marshmallows. Refrigerate till serving time.

SEAFOAM SALAD

1 pkg. lime Jello	1 pkg. Dream Whip
1 C. pear juice	Large can pears
3 oz. pkg. cream cheese	1 pkg. orange Jello
2 T. coffee cream	

    Dissolve lime Jello in 1 C. hot pear juice. While mixture is hot, add cream cheese and coffee cream. Let thicken a little and add whipped Dream Whip and can of mashed pears. Let set. Top with orange Jello dissolved, according to package directions.

MAIN DISHES

HAM BALLS

2½ lb. ground ham
2 lb. ground pork
1 lb. ground beef
3 eggs, beaten
⅔ C. crushed graham crackers
1½ to 2 C. milk

1 tsp. salt (optional)
2 cans tomato soup
2¼ C. brown sugar
¾ C. vinegar
2 tsp. dry mustard

Combine meats, eggs, cracker crumbs, milk and salt, if desired and mix well. Using ½ C. measuring cup, form 25 small ham loaves. Place in pan and cover with sauce. Make a sauce of soup, brown sugar, vinegar and mustard; don't cook. Pour over meat and bake 1 hour at 350°. This makes a large amount. May be divided and frozen.

MUSHROOM STEAK BAKE

1 can or 2 env. mushroom soup
1 T. instant minced onion

1 4-lb. chuck roast (beef)

Combine soup mix (dry) and onion on a sheet of heavy foil. Roll roast in mixture to coat well then wrap loosely, sealing edges well. Place on cookie sheet. Bake in 350° oven for 3 hours. Reset oven to broil. Slit foil across top and fold back being careful not to let gravy run out. Broil roast 5 minutes. Carve and serve with gravy from foil.

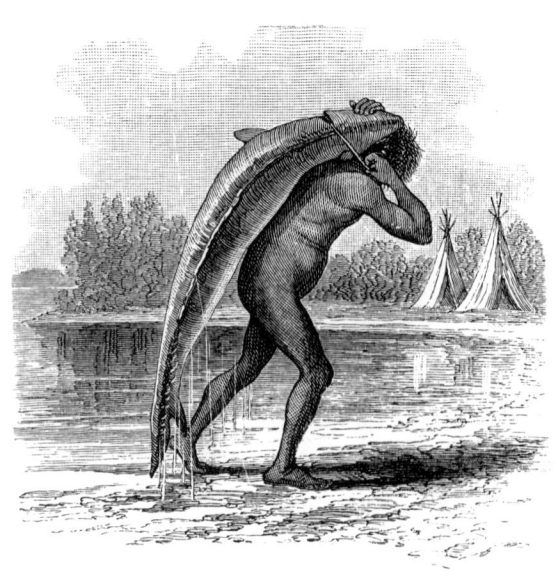

BAKED PINEAPPLE

1 No. 2½ can crushed pineapple
2 rounded T. flour
¼ to ½ lb. grated Cheddar or or Longhorn cheese
1 scant C. sugar
½ tsp. salt
Buttered crumbs

    Mix sugar, flour and salt. Add pineapple (do not drain juice off pineapple). Add grated cheese. Pour into buttered baking dish and cover with buttered crumbs. Bake at 350° for about 40 minutes or until brown on top. This makes 8 to 12 servings.

TEXAS YUMMY (Serves 15-20)

2 lb. ground beef (browned)
2 T. sugar
Dash of pepper
2 tsp. salt
2 cloves garlic
1 6-oz. can tomato paste
1 can tomato soup

SECOND LAYER:
1 12-oz. pkg. noodles, cooked
1 T. oleo
6 green onions, chopped
1 pt. sour cream
1 8-oz. pkg. cream cheese

THIRD LAYER:
½ C. Parmesan cheese
1 C. grated Cheddar cheese

    Layer in pan as ingredients are listed, topping noodles with the cheese. Bake in oven 25-30 minutes.

PORK CHOPS IN CROCK POT

4 medium pork chops
Salt & pepper
5-8 potatoes (peeled & chopped)
½ C. onion (chopped)
1 can Cheddar cheese soup
½ C. milk

Place potatoes, soup, milk and onions in the crock pot. Add salt and pepper and stir all together. Place seasoned pork chops on top. Cook on low for 6-8 hours.

SWISS STEAK

1½ lb. round or rump beef (1½" thick)
2 T. flour
1 tsp. salt
1/8 tsp. pepper
2 T. salad oil
1½ C. canned tomatoes
3 large peeled onions (slice thin)
1 stalk celery, diced
1 minced clove garlic
1 T. bottled meat sauce A1 or Heinz
¼ C. raisins

Trim excess fat off meat. Combine flour, salt and pepper. Lay beef on bread board. Spread it with ½ of flour mixture then pound in with rim of saucer. Turn over and pound in remaining flour mixture. Heat salad oil in heavy skillet or Dutch oven. Brown meat well on both sides on medium heat. Add rest of ingredients. Stir well; cover and simmer 1¾ to 2 hours or until meat is tender. Skim off fat if necessary.

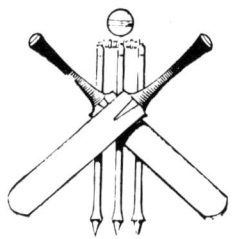

DEVILED STEAK

1 C. tomato juice
½ C. water
1 T. lemon juice or vinegar
1 T. Worcestershire sauce
1 tsp. celery seed
1 tsp. dry mustard
1 small grated onion

Brown the steak, pour sauce over and cook in oven until tender.

SWEET AND SOUR PORK

1½ lb. lean pork shoulder (cubed)
#2 can pineapple chunks
¼ C. brown sugar
2 T. cornstarch
¼ C. vinegar
1 T. soy sauce
½ tsp. salt
¾ C. green pepper, strips
¼ C. onions, thinly sliced

Brown pork cubes in hot fat. Add ¼ C. water. Cover and simmer until tender, about 1 hour. Drain pineapple, reserving syrup. Combine brown sugar and cornstarch and add pineapple syrup, vinegar, soy sauce and salt. Cook and stir over low heat until thick. Pour over hot pork that has been cooked. Let stand 10 minutes. Add pineapple chunks, green pepper strips and onion slices. Cook a few minutes until green pepper and onions are tender. Serves 5. Excellent served over rice or in a chafing dish as hors d'oeuvres.

LUAU LOIN

5 lb. boned pork loin

SAUCE:
1 7¾-oz. jar baby food peaches
⅓ C. ketchup
½ C. brown sugar
1/8 tsp. garlic powder
⅓ C. cider vinegar
1 T. soy sauce

Stir above into a small saucepan. Bring to a boil, stirring frequently. Place loin on rotisserie. Grill approximately 15 minutes per pound. One-half hour before loin is done, brush with Luau sauce. Repeat 5 minutes before removing loin.

BAKED CHICKEN

4 C. bread cubes	1 tsp. sage
1 C. whole milk	Dash of pepper
2 beaten eggs	1 heaping qt. diced salted chicken
2 tsp. salt	

Mix bread cubes and milk; add eggs, salt, sage, pepper and chicken. Mix well. Make gravy of broth and pour over top. Bake in 350° oven for 35 minutes.

CLEONE'S LASAGNA

2 cloves garlic, minced	1 tsp. oregano
1½ lb. ground beef	½ lb. Mozzarella cheese
1 box lasagna noodles (8 oz.)	1 lb. cottage cheese
1 can (15 oz.) tomato sauce	2 T. Parmesan cheese
1 can (12 oz.) tomato paste	1 pkg. dry onion soup
½ tsp. salt & sugar	2 T. cooking oil
¼ tsp. pepper	

Cook lasagna noodles according to package. Add 2 T. oil to cooking oil. Drain and put in cool water until ready to use. Brown garlic and ground beef. Add onion soup, tomato paste and tomato sauce, salt, sugar, pepper and oregano. Simmer 30 minutes. Stir occasionally. Put small amount of meat sauce in bottom of pan. Put a layer of noodles, mozzarella cheese and cottage cheese. Repeat ending with sauce on top. Sprinkle with Parmesan cheese. Bake at 350° for 30 minutes.

CHICKEN AND RICE

Uncooked bacon
6 or 8 pieces of chicken
1 C. uncooked rice
1 can cream of chicken soup
1 can water
Garlic salt
Pepper
Parsley flakes
Oregano

Cover bottom of greased baking dish with pieces of uncooked bacon. Put chicken pieces on top of bacon and leave a hole in the middle. Put rice in hole. Pour cream of chicken soup over rice - spread some on top of chicken. Add 1 can of water. Makes holes in rice pile so water and soup can soak int. Sprinkle garlic salt, pepper, parsley flakes and oregano on top. Cover and bake at 350° for 1 hour or until done. May have to add more water to rice. Stir rice once or twice.

SAUSAGE CASSEROLE

8 slices bread (cubed)
1½ lb. ground pork sausage
2 C. grated cheese, cheddar or other
1 can (4 oz.) mushrooms, drained
4 eggs, beaten
¾ tsp. dry mustard
2½ C. milk
1 can cream of mushroom soup
½ C. milk

Fry and drain sausage. Place cubed bread in bottom of a 9 x 13-inch greased pan. Layer sausage, cheese and mushrooms. Mix eggs, mustard and milk. Pour over dish and refrigerate. Just before baking mix mushroom soup with milk and pour over top of casserole. Bake at 300° for 1½ hours.

BACON QUICHE

12 slices crumbled bacon
1 C. Swiss or Cheddar cheese
⅓ C. chopped onion
2 C. milk
1 C. Bisquick
4 eggs
¼ tsp. salt
1/8 tsp. pepper

Into a 10" greased pie plate, sprinkle bacon, shredded cheese and onion. Beat milk, Bisquick, eggs, salt and pepper with mixer until smooth. Pour over other ingredients. Bake at 400° for 35 minutes. Let stand. Serves 4 to 6 people.

SAUSAGE AND EGG CASSEROLE

½ lb. sharp Cheddar cheese (grated)
½ lb. Swiss cheese (grated)
1½ lb. sausage (browned & drained)
3¼ C. milk
8 eggs, beaten
½ tsp. salt
Bread slices

Cover entire bottom of 9 x 13-inch pan with bread slices (remove crust). Put grated cheese on bread, then add sausage. Pour milk, egg and salt mixture over top. Refrigerate overnight. Can use 1 lb. crumbled bacon instead of sausage. Bake at 350° for 45 minutes.

BURGER BUNDLES

1 lb. hamburger (seasoned)
⅓ C. condensed milk
1 box dressing mix
1 C. hot water (approx.)

1 can cream of mushroom soup
Water (small amount)
1 T. catsup
2 tsp. Worcestershire sauce

Combine hamburger and milk and form into burgers. Mix dressing mix and hot water until moist. Wrap around the burgers on top and bottom and place in baking dish. Mix together mushroom soup, water, catsup and Worcestershire sauce and heat to boiling point and pour over bundles and bake 40 minutes in a slow oven at 325°.

HAMBURGER PIE

1 lb. hamburger
Salt & pepper
⅔ C. peas

1 can tomato soup
Mashed potatoes
Cheddar cheese

Brown hamburger, salt and pepper. Add peas and 1 can tomato soup. Put in 1½ quart baking dish. Top with mashed potatoes. Sprinkle with Cheddar cheese. Bake at 350° for 35-40 minutes.

DESSERTS

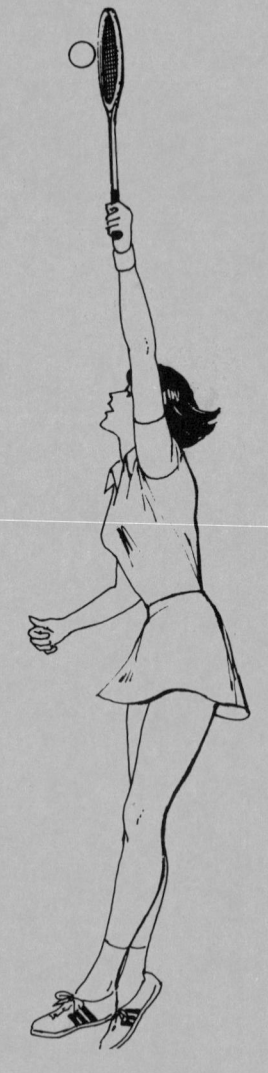

RHUBARB DESSERT OR RHUBARB CRUNCH

4 C. chopped rhubarb
1 to 1½ C. sugar
1 pkg. strawberry Jello (dry)
1 pkg. Jiffy yellow or white cake mix or reg. size

Cinnamon & ginger (optional)
¼ to ¾ C. melted oleo
½ to 1 C. water

Place rhubarb in a greased 9 x 13-inch baking dish. Sprinkle sugar over rhubarb and then dry Jello. Next, layer cake mix over rhubarb mixture. Sprinkle with cinnamon and ginger if desired. Drizzle melted oleo over cake mix and pour water over top. Bake in a 325° to 350° oven for 40 to 55 minutes. May be served with cream, whipped cream or ice cream if desired.

CHOCOLATE ICE CREAM

4 eggs
3½ C. sugar
¾ C. cocoa (sifted)
½ tsp. salt
3 C. milk

2 T. vanilla
4 C. cream
Milk to fill freezer can
4 junket tablets
(dissolved in 4 T. water)

Beat eggs; gradually add sugar, cocoa and salt. Beat until sugar is dissolved. Add milk and heat until mixture reaches a scald. Remove from heat and add vanilla. Pour into freezer can; add cream and milk to fill can. Then add the junket tablets that have been dissolved in water. Stir slightly. Put on lid and wait 10 minutes before freezing.

SCANDINAVIAN RICE PUDDING

2 C. milk
½ C. uncooked rice
½ C. light or heavy cream
1 tsp. vanilla

1/8 tsp. salt
⅓ C. sugar
2 T. butter

In the top of a double boiler or in the server part of a rice cooker, heat milk; stir in rice. Cover and cook over boiling water, stirring occasionally as mixture thickens and adding milk if necessary, until rice is tender 1 to 1½ hours. Stir in cream, vanilla, salt, sugar and butter. Remove from heat and allow to stand over hot water until ready to serve. The mixture will thicken as it stands. This recipe doubles well.

APRICOT SHERBET

1 size 2½ can apricots (pureed)
Juice of 2 lemons
3 C. sugar

2 to 2½ C. cream
Milk to fill can

Puree apricots and add the rest of the ingredients. Stir until well blended and pour into freezer can. Add milk to fill can. Makes 1½ gallons.

CHOCOLATE TOPPING

2 C. boiling water
1 C. sugar
1 (heaping) T. cocoa

1 (heaping) T. flour
1 tsp. vanilla

Mix together sugar, cocoa, flour and vanilla. Add boiling water, stir until well blended. Bring to a boil and boil for 4 minutes. Good warm over cake or ice cream.

DIGESTION AID

APPETIZERS & BEVERAGES

CHEESE BALL

1 lg. pkg. Phil. cream cheese
1 jar Kraft pimento cheese
Onion salt, to taste
Celery salt, to taste
Garlic salt, to taste
1 jar Kraft Cheddar cheese
(English sharp)

Mix all ingredients well and roll in crushed pecans. Keep in refrigerator until ready to serve.

BLACK OLIVE CHEESE BALL

1 (8 oz.) pkg. cream cheese
1 (16 oz.) pkg. sharp Cheddar cheese (grated)
1 can black olives (sliced)
1 sm. container smoked cheese
1 tsp. minced onion

Blend cheese together; add olives and form into ball. Garnish with nuts or olives.

CORN FRITTERS

1 C. corn
1 T. flour
3 egg yolks
1 tsp. salt

Mix together. Beat egg whites and fold in. Fry in butter.

HOT CIDER PUNCH

4 C. apple juice
4 C. water
1 C. pre-sweetened strawberry or cherry Kool-Aid mix
¼ tsp. cinnamon
1/8 tsp. nutmeg & cloves

Mix well and bring to a boil. Serve hot. Approximately serves 16.

CHEESE BALL

16 oz. cream cheese
8 oz. can crushed pineapple (drained)
2 T. chopped onion
½ C. green pepper (chopped)
1 T. Lawry's salt
1 C. pecans (chopped)
1 C. pecans (broken)

Mix all, but the last cup of pecans for the cheese ball. Use last cup of pecans to decorate outside of ball.

CRANBERRY TEA

2 C. water
1½ C. sugar
½ bag red hots
1 qt. cranberry juice

2 C. orange juice
2 T. lemon juice
6 cloves

Boil water, sugar and red hots until candies melt. Mix the rest and serve warm, or can store in refrigerator and serve cold. Can use 1 quart cranberries and 1 qt. water, cooked and strained. Then cook 1 quart water, 3 C. sugar, 6 cloves and ½ C. red hots. Combine this with juice of 3 oranges and 3 lemons.

ORANGE JULIUS

1 6-oz. can frozen orange juice (undiluted)
1 6-oz. can of milk
1 6-oz. can water

½ C. powdered sugar
1 tsp. vanilla
6-12 ice cubes

Put all ingredients in blender until smooth. Can use 2 cans of milk, instead of water.

PINEAPPLE CHEESE BALL

2 (8 oz. ea.) pkgs. cream cheese
1 chopped green pepper
½ C. green onion
8½ oz. can crushed pineapple (well drained)
Walnuts or pecans

Mix together and chill 1 hour, then form into ball. Roll in chopped walnuts or pecans.

RUSSIAN TEA

2 C. Tang
¼ C. powdered lemonade
¼ C. instant tea
3 C. sugar
1½ tsp. cloves
1½ tsp. cinnamon

Mix altogether. I use 3 tsp. for each cup of hot water.

SLUSH

2 pkg. Kool-Aid
2 C. sugar
3 qt. water
1 6-oz. can frozen orange juice
1 6-oz. can frozen lemonade
1 qt. gingerale

Freeze. Then set out in room temperature for about 6-8 hours until slushy.

CANDY & COOKIES

*EASY APRICOT DAINTIES

1 lb. dried apricots
1 orange, peeled
2 C. sugar

Soak apricots in warm water. (Don't let them get too soft.) Remove bitter white skin from peel of orange and membrane from pulp. Put orange (rind and pulp) and apricots through food grinder. Add sugar. Boil 8 minutes or until mixture drops in large blobs from a spoon. Cool slightly. Drop from teaspoon into bowl of sugar and roll into balls. Cool on waxed paper.

CARAMELS

1 C. oleo or butter
1 lb. brown sugar (2½ C.)
Dash salt
1 C. light corn syrup
1 15-oz. can sweetened cond. milk
1 tsp. vanilla

Melt butter in heavy 3 quart saucepan. Add brown sugar and salt. Stir till thoroughly combined. Blend in corn syrup. Gradually add sweetened condensed milk, stirring constantly. Cook and stir over medium heat till candy reaches firm ball stage. Stir in vanilla. Pour in buttered 13 x 9-inch pan. Cool and cut, wrap in waxed paper.

DIPPED PRETZELS

1 pkg. white almond bark
Pretzels

Melt 1 pkg. of white almond bark in 200° oven. Dip pretzels in warm bark and lay on waxed paper to cool.

KARO CRUNCH

2 qt. popped corn
1½ C. chopped pecans
⅔ C. slivered almonds
1⅓ C. sugar
1 C. butter
½ C. Karo syrup
1 tsp. vanilla

    Combine popcorn, pecans, almond on a cookie sheet, with sides. Mix well. In a saucepan, combine sugar, butter and syrup. Bring to boil over medium heat, stirring occasionally, for 10 to 15 minutes or until it turns a caramel color. Remove from heat. Stir in vanilla. Pour over popcorn mixture; mix to coat well. Cool and store in airtight container.

PEANUT BUTTER CANDY

3 C. sugar
1½ C. milk
3 T. butter or oleo
3 heaping T. peanut butter

    Boil sugar, milk and oleo until mixture makes softball. Take off heat and beat in the peanut butter.

CRACKER JACK CARAMEL CORN

½ of a 10 oz. can of corn
2 C. brown sugar, firmly packed
Pinch of baking soda
3 T. corn syrup
½ C. butter or margarine

    Cook together the sugar, butter and syrup, stirring constantly, until it brittles in cold water. Remove from heat and add a pinch of baking soda. Add corn which has been popped. Stir with a fork until well coated. Put out on a cookie sheet to cool.

BREADS

KRUMKAKE

3 eggs
½ C. flour
½ C. melted butter
½ C. sugar
1 tsp. vanilla or lemon extract

Mix all ingredients. Bake in Krumkake iron until golden brown. Roll on cone while warm to shape.

ICE BOX MUFFINS

1 C. boiling water
½ C. Crisco
1½ C. sugar
2½ C. flour
½ tsp. salt
1 C. bran buds
2 eggs
1 pt. buttermilk
2½ tsp. soda
2 C. all bran

Mix boiling water and 1 cup bran buds. Combine Crisco, eggs, sugar and buttermilk. Add flour, soda, salt and all bran. Drop desired amount in muffin tins and bake 15 minutes at 400°. May be kept in refrigerator for 3 weeks and dropped in muffin tins without further beating.

WALNUT LEMON MUFFINS

1¾ C. flour
½ C. sugar
3 tsp. baking powder
½ tsp. salt
⅔ C. chopped walnuts

1 egg
⅔ C. milk
½ tsp. grated lemon peel
1 tsp. lemon juice
⅓ C. melted shortening

Combine and bake.

BAKING POWDER BISCUITS

2 C. flour
4 tsp. baking powder
½ tsp. cream of tartar
½ tsp. salt

2 T. sugar
½ C. shortening
⅔ C. milk
1 egg

Sift dry ingredients; blend in shortening and pour milk in slowly. Add egg, knead and roll ½-inch thickness. Put on ungreased sheet. Bake 10-15 minutes at 350°.

NEVER FAIL DUMPLINGS

1½ C. flour
Pinch of salt
4 C. milk

1 tsp. baking powder
1 egg

Mix well and drop into broth. Keep covered 5-6 minutes. Cook 1-2 minutes longer.

PUFFY BAKED PANCAKES

½ C. flour
1 tsp. vanilla
4 T. butter
½ fresh lemon (optional)

½ C. milk
2 eggs
2 T. powdered sugar

This goes very fast. Preheat oven to 425°. Lightly beat flour, milk, vanilla and eggs together. Batter should be lumpy. Melt butter in 10-12 inch skillet, until pan and butter are very hot and pour batter in. Bake 15-20 minutes until puffy and golden. Sprinkle top of pancake with confectioner's sugar and drops of lemon juice if desired. Serve immediately. Alternate topping: Whipped cream type topping and sliced fresh strawberries or other fruit.

HOME-MADE NOODLES

4 eggs
1 tsp. salt

¼ tsp. baking powder
Flour

Combine ingredients using enough flour to make a stiff dough. Roll out thin and let dough dry for 1 to 2 hours. Cut and add to chicken or beef broth.

BAKED PANCAKE

2 eggs	⅓ C. flour
½ tsp. salt	½ C. milk
2 T. sugar	½ tsp. fat

Beat eggs, salt and sugar. Add flour and milk and beat until smooth. Heat fat in deep skillet (10-12" diameter) until a drop of water sizzles. Pour in batter and cook 2 minutes on top of stove. Bake about 15 minutes at 450° or until surface is golden brown. Butter and serve with syrup or sugar.

BRAN MUFFINS

1¼ C. flour	3 tsp. baking powder
½ tsp. salt	⅓ C. sugar
1 C. bran buds cereal	1 C. milk
¼ C. shortening	1 egg

Stir together flour, baking powder, salt and sugar; set aside. Measure bran buds and milk into mixing bowl. Stir to combine. Let stand 1-2 minutes. Add egg and shortening and beat well. Add dry ingredients to cereal mixture, stirring only until combined. Bake at 400° for about 25 minutes or until brown. Serve hot. Yeild 12 muffins.

VEGGIES

BROCCOLI CASSEROLE

3 pkg. frozen broccoli spears
1 can cream of mushroom soup
1 can milk (use soup can)
Grated Longhorn cheese
Crumbled Ritz crackers

Cook broccoli in salted water until tender. Drain and place in casserole dish. Mix soup and milk together and add to broccoli. Place fairly thick layer of cheese on top of that, then a layer of crackers. Sprinkle with pepper and dot with butter. Bake uncovered at 350° for 45 minutes.

BROCCOLI-CORN CASSEROLE (Serves 6;

1 lb. can creamed style corn
1 10-oz. pkg. frozen, chopped broccoli (cooked & drained)
1 egg, beaten
½ C. coarse saltine cracker crumbs
¼ C. chopped onion
3 T. oleo, melted
½ tsp. salt
Dash of pepper
1 C. bread or cracker crumbs
2 T. oleo, melted

In mixing bowl, beat egg; add corn, cooked broccoli, cracker crumbs, onion, 3 T. melted oleo, salt and pepper. Turn into 1 quart casserole. Combine the 1 C. bread or cracker crumbs and 2 T. oleo, melted and sprinkle over top of vegetables. BAke uncovered at 350° for 35-40 minutes or until heated through.

BROCCOLI-GREEN CHILI DELIGHT (Serves 6)

⅔ C. diced onion	½ soup can of milk
⅔ C. diced celery	1 C. water
2 T. cooking oil	1 C. instant rice (uncooked)
1 10-oz. pkg. frozen broccoli (thawed)	1 can Cheddar cheese soup
1 can cream of mushroom soup	1 C. chopped green chilies

Saute onion and celery in oil. Add thawed broccoli. Simmer 15 minutes. Add soup, milk, water, rice, cheese and chilies. Bring to a boil. Pour into buttered 1½ quart casserole. Bake 25 minutes or until well heated.

SCALLOPED CABBAGE (Use Large Oblong Pan)

1 large head cabbage
1 can cream of mushroom soup
   thinned with ½ can milk
8 oz. pkg. grated Cheddar cheese
1½ C. crushed potato chips

Layer raw cabbage, mushroom soup and cheese. Top with crumbs. Bake at 350° for 35 minutes.

BROCCOLI DISH

1 box frozen broccoli
1 can cream of mushroom soup
1 can cream of chicken soup
1½ C. Minute Rice (not cooked)
8 oz. jar Cheez Whiz

Partly thaw broccoli and break up in pieces. Mix other ingredients with broccoli and stir. Place in casserole dish and bake at 350° for 45-60 minutes.

ESCALLOPED BROCCOLI BAKE (Serves 6-8)

1½ lbs. fresh broccoli spears (or 2 pkg. frozen)
1 can cream of mushroom soup
¼ C. milk
½ C. shredded Cheddar cheese
1 C. Bisquick
¼ C. butter

Heat 1-inch salted water (½ tsp. salt to 1 C. water) to boiling. Add broccoli. Cover and heat to boiling. Cook until almost tender (10 to 12 minutes) and drain. Place broccoli in ungreased 1½ quart round casserole. Heat oven to 400°. Beat soup and milk until smooth. Pour over broccoli. Sprinkle with cheese. Mix Bisquick and butter until crumbly. Sprinkle over cheese. Bake until crumbs are light brown, about 20 minutes. Frozn cauliflower may be substituted for broccoli.

ESCALLOPED CABBAGE

Cabbage
3 T. flour
Salt & pepper, to taste
Bread crumbs
¼ C. butter
2 C. milk
½ lb. Velveeta cheese

Cook cabbage in salt water until tender; drain. Make white sauce of butter, flour, milk, salt, pepper and cheese. Pour this over cabbage. Cover with dried bread crumbs. Bake at 350° for 35 minutes. (Can use broccoli or asparagus in place of cabbage.)

COOKED CABBAGE WITH SWEET AND SOUR DRESSING

1 med. size head cabbage
1 egg (beaten with pinch of salt)
1 T. sugar
Butter (size of egg)
3 T. sweet cream
3 T. apple cider vinegar

Cut up cabbage and cook in boiling water until tender. Drain thoroughly. Add a chunk of butter the size of an egg. Add dressing ingredients to the hot cabbage, and cook until egg is thoroughly cooked. Then it is ready to serve.

COMPANY CARROTS

4 C. sliced carrots (cooked)
⅓ stick oleo
1 large onion (chopped)
½ lb. shredded Velveeta cheese

    Saute onion in oleo. Put carrots, onions and cheese in a buttered casserole dish. Top with cornflakes or potato chip crumbs. Bake at 350° for 30 minutes.

SAUCY CELERY CASSEROLE

4 C. thinly sliced celery
¼ C. butter or oleo
2 T. flour
1 C. milk
2 T. chopped pimento
1 C. shredded sharp American cheese
¼ tsp. salt
4 ozs. mushrooms (chop & drain)
2 T. chopped green peppers

    Cook celery in butter until tender. Stir in salt and flour. Add milk, cook until thick and bubbly. Add ¾ C. cheese, stir until melted. Stir in mushrooms, pepper and pimento. Turn into 1 quart casserole. Bake uncovered at 350° for 20 minutes. Sprinkle with remaining cheese.

SOUPS & SANDWICHES

CHEESESQUARES

1 loaf sandwich bread
2 sticks butter or margarine
2 jars Old English sharp cheese
½ tsp. Tobasco sauce
1 tsp. dill weed
¾ tsp. Beau Monde
¾ tsp. Worcestershire sauce
Dash of cayenne pepper

Freeze bread, take out and sort in 3 slice groups and cut off crusts. Spread cheese mixture over each slice and cut in quarters. Frost each quarter with cheese mixture. Put on greased cookie sheet and freeze. Remove from freezer 20 minutes before serving and put in oven at 350° for 20 minutes. Serve immediately.

CANDLELIGHT STEW

2 lbs. beef stew meat
2 T. salad oil
Salt & pepper
1 (10 oz.) can cream of mushroom soup
⅓ C. burgundy wine (alcohol cooks off but leaves flavor)
1 (8 oz.) can sliced mushrooms
2 T. dry onion soup mix
1 medium carrot (peeled & shredded)

Brown meat in hot salad oil. Salt and pepper, to taste. Transfer to 2-quart baking dish. Combine remaining ingredients and pour over meat. Bake, covered at 350° for about 2 hours or until meat is tender, stirring occasionally as it bakes. Add small amount of beef broth if you like more gravy. Serves 6.

BRUNSWICK STEW

1 chicken (about 4 lbs.)
4 C. water
4 slices bacon
½ lb. lean hamburger
1 small onion (minced)
1¼ tsp. salt
1 tsp. paprika
1¾ to 2 C. (1 lb. can) tomatoes

1 pkg. (10 oz.) frozen lima beans
1½ to 2 C. (12 oz. can) whole kernel corn
3 medium potatoes (diced)
Seasoned salt & pepper
All-purpose flour
Any good bar-b-que sauce

Boil chicken until done, cool, remove meat from bones, reserving broth and cut into bite-sized pieces. Dice bacon and brown in kettle. Remove bacon and brown hamburger and onion in fat remaining in kettle. Add bacon, chicken broth, salt, paprika and tomatoes. Bring to boil, cover and simmer for 1½ hours. Add remaining chicken and simmer 30 minutes longer. Season to taste with bar-b-que sauce and thicken slightly with flour and water paste.

CHILI

1 lb. hamburger
2 small onions (chopped)
2 cans tomato soup or tomatoes
2 cans water

2 cans kidney beans
1 T. chili powder
Shortening, size of walnut
Salt & pepper, to taste

Brown hamburger in shortening and onion; drain. Add salt and pepper. Add beans, tomato soup and water; simmer.

SHREDDED BEEF SANDWICHES

1 (3 lb.) beef chuck pot roast
⅓ C. vinegar
1 large onion (cut-up)
3 bay leaves

½ tsp. salt
¼ tsp. ground cloves
1/8 tsp. garlic powder
8 to 10 French rolls (split)

Trim fat from roast. Cut meat as necessary to fit into a 3 or 4 quart electric slow cooker, place meat in cooker. Combine vinegar, onion, bay leaves, salt, cloves and garlic powder; pour over meat. Cover and cook on low heat, stirring for 11 to 12 hours or till meat is very tender. Remove meat and use two forks to shred meat. Discard bones and fat. Makes 8 to 10 servings.

SALADS

TACO SALAD

1 lb. hamburger
1 head lettuce (cut-up)
1 small onion
Tomatoes

Shredded cheese
Russian dressing
Taco chips

Cook hamburger and cool. Add vegetables and cheese, mixing thoroughly. Add the dressing and broken chips just before serving.

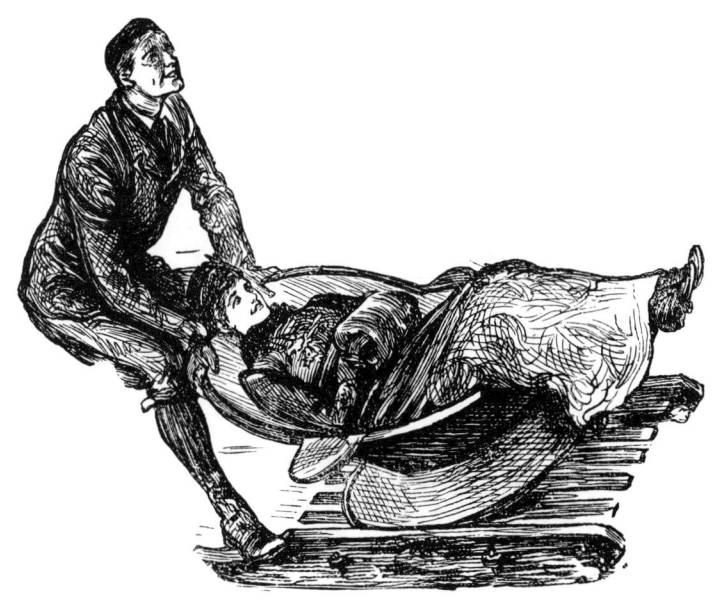

TUNA SALAD

1 C. cheese, cubed
2 eggs, hard boiled & chopped
1 can tuna
2 T. green pepper, chopped

2 T. onion, minced
2 T. sweet pickles, diced
½ C. celery, diced
1 C. canned or frozen peas

Moisten ingredients with ¼ C. mayonnaise plus 1 T. lemon juice. Serves 6. Serve with a variety of crackers.

TUNA-MACARONI SALAD

3 C. cooked, drained macaroni
6 hard-boiled eggs, chopped
1 7-oz. can chunk tuna, separated
1 heaping T. sweet relish
3 sweet chopped pickles
3 tsp. sugar
Miracle Whip

Cream Miracle Whip and sugar. Mix with rest of ingredients and refrigerate.

DUTCH LETTUCE SALAD

7 or 8 med. sized potatoes (boiled)
4 or 5 C. leaf or head lettuce
7 or 8 strips bacon
   (cut in small pieces)
6 eggs (boiled)
1 C. green onion (tops & all)
⅓ C. vinegar
Salt & pepper, to taste

Boil potatoes until tender. Cut lettuce and onion in small pieces in large bowl. Fry small pieces of bacon until crisp and add vinegar. Mash potatoes sparingly and add cut up boiled eggs. Pour bacon and vinegar mixture over lettuce and onion and add potatoes and eggs. Mix altogether. Delicious as a one-dish meal.

SALAD IN A BAG

1 head lettuce
8 radishes
2 stalks celery
2 medium tomatoes
2 carrots
½ C. favorite salad dressing

Wash and prepare the lettuce, tomatoes, radishes, carrots and celery and put in a plastic bag. Pour in the salad dressing, close the bag and tie it tightly. Shake once or twice and empty into a salad bowl.

TOSSED SALAD

Lettuce
4 slices bacon
Mayonnaise
Cooked peas
4 eggs, hard boiled
Swiss cheese, shredded

Use oblong pan: A layer of lettuce, a layer of cooked peas, bacon crumbled over top, eggs, sliced. Cover with real mayonnaise, sprinkle top with spreaded Swiss cheese. Cover and let stand in refrigerator all day or overnight.

THREE-BEAN SALAD

1 can green beans
1 can wax beans
1 can kidney beans
1 medium onion, sliced
½ C. sugar
⅓ C. salad oil
⅓ C. vinegar
½ tsp. salt
½ tsp. pepper
½ tsp. celery salt

Store in air-tight covered bowl.

BEAN SALAD

1 16-oz. can dark red kidney beans (drained & rinsed)
1 16-oz. can chili beans (drained & rinsed)
3 hard boiled eggs
4 med. sized pickles
1/8 C. onion
Salt, pepper & mayonnaise to taste

Mix all ingredients together.

CABBAGE SALAD

6 C. finely shredded cabbage
2 med. carrots, shredded
1 small onion, grated
½ green pepper, chopped
¾ C. oil
⅓ C. vinegar
⅓ C. water
1 C. sugar
¼ tsp. mustard seed
1 tsp. salt
1 tsp. celery seed
1 pkg. lemon Jello

Combine vegetables and pour oil over them. Let stand while heating vinegar, water, sugar, mustard seed, salt and celery seed. Stir well to dissolve and bring to a boil. Remove from stove and add 1 pkg. lemon Jello. Stir well. Let cool, but not set. Pour over oil and vegetables. Mix well and refrigerate at least overnight. This salad keeps well for a couple of weeks.

CHICKEN SALAD

2 C. cooked diced chicken
1 C. cooked frozen peas
1 C. diced celery
½ tsp. salt
¼ tsp. curry powder
1 tsp. grated onion
1/8 tsp. pepper
½ C. Hellman's mayonnaise
½ C. slivered almonds

Mix and chill.

CHEESE SALAD

1 pkg. lemon Jello
1 C. Miracle Whip
1 C. Cheddar cheese, grated
1 T. vinegar (optional)
Pimento or red pepper (chopped)
Salt, to taste
Onion juice or minced onion to taste

Dissolve Jello in 2 C. water. Let stand until nearly firm. Beat in ½ Miracle Whip at a time. Whip until light and fluffy. Fold in the other ingredients and chill.

MARINATED CARROTS

2 lb. fresh carrots
1 large onion, sliced in rings
1 large green pepper, cut in strips
1 can tomato soup, undiluted
1 C. sugar
½ C. salad oil
¾ C. vinegar
1 tsp. salt
½ tsp. pepper
¼ tsp. dill weed

Wash, peel and cut carrots into 1" pieces. Cook until just tender. Drain and cool. Combine soup, sugar, oil, vinegar, salt and pepper. Pour hot soup mixture over vegetables. Sprinkle with dill weed and cover and chill in refrigerator overnight.

CARROT-CHEESE SALAD

½ C. diced celery
2 C. cottage cheese
1 C. shredded carrots
1 C. drained pineapple
1 tsp. lemon juice
½ C. Miracle Whip
2 T. sugar

Mix Miracle Whip and sugar and add to shredded carrots. Then toss in other ingredients. This can be fixed ahead of serving time.

MARINATED CARROTS

2 lb. carrots (sliced)
½ large onion, cut in rings
½ green pepper, cut in strips
1 8-oz. can tomato sauce
½ C. vinegar
1 C. sugar
½ tsp. Worcestershire sauce

Cook carrots in salted water until tender. Drain and cool. Mix all ingredients together and let set overnight.

GERMAN STYLE WILTED LETTUCE

6 C. leaf lettuce (torn in bite size pieces)
2 eggs, hard cooked & diced
⅓ C. chopped (Bermuda) onion
4 slices bacon
½ tsp. salt
1 T. sugar
3 T. cider vinegar

Cook bacon until lightly browned. Remove and drain, then crumble over lettuce. Cool fat slightly and add sugar, salt and vinegar. Heat to boiling and pour over lettuce. Toss lightly. Serve immediately.

CABBAGE SALAD

Head of cabbage, chopped.
2 carrots, shredded
1 medium onion, diced
½ green or red pepper
1 tsp. celery seed
1 T. salt

SAUCE:
1¼ C. sugar
¾ C. salad oil
¾ C. vinegar

Stir and boil sauce. Pour over cabbage while hot. Stir after it has cooled.

HEARTHSIDE SALAD

1 head cauliflower (cut in bite size pieces)
2 C. white grapes (cut & seeded)
4 stalks celery (in bite size pieces)
½ to 1 C. pecan nutmeats

DRESSING:
1 C. Hellman's mayonnaise
½ C. sugar
2 T. prepared mustard

Mix and let stand awhile so sugar will be dissolved. Add dressing to salad just before serving.

CAULIFLOWER-PEA SALAD

2 C. chopped cauliflower
1 C. diced celery
2 C. frozen peas (cooked & cooled)
Chopped onion, to taste
½ pkg. Hidden Valley garlic dressing
1 C. Miracle Whip or Light & Lively for fewer calories

Combine vegetables with dressing by tossing. The salad lasts for several days and the flavor of the onions and dressings gets stronger. Be sure to store in covered bowl in refrigerator.

CHICKEN SALAD

4 C. diced cooked chicken
1 small green pepper, chopped
½ C. stuffed olives, chopped
1 C. pineapple tidbits, drained
1 C. mandarin oranges, drained
1 pt. Miracle Whip
2 oz. salad mustard
¼ medium size red onion, chopped

Mix all ingredients together and chill overnight. Before serving; add 1 large can Chinese noodles.

GREEN AND WHITE VEGETABLE SALAD

1 bunch fresh broccoli
1 medium cauliflower, broken
1½ C. chopped celery
6 green onions, chopped fine
¾ C. Miracle Whip
¼ C. whipping cream
2 T. sugar
1 tsp. salt
¼ tsp. pepper

    Remove large leaves of broccoli and cut off tough ends; wash and cut into 1-inch pieces. Combine vegetables in large bowl. Mix remaining ingredients. Pour over vegetables and toss lightly to coat. Cover and chill thoroughly. Makes 8-10 servings.

CARROT OR CABBAGE SALAD

1 pkg. Jello
2 C. boiling water
3 oz. cream cheese
1 pkg. Dream Whip
1 C. carrot or cabbage, grated
1 can pineapple, drained

    Mix and let almost set, the first three ingredients. Whip the Dream Whip and add the carrots or cabbage and pineapple. Beat in Jello and let set.

TUNA CRUNCH SALAD

1 6-oz. can tuna, drained
¼ C. chopped sweet pickles
1 T. minced onion
1-2 T. lemon juice
¾ C. salad dressing
1½ C. shredded cabbage
1½ C. crushed potato chips

    Combine first 5 ingredients. Cover and chill until ready to serve. Add cabbage and toss. Add 1 C. crushed potato chips and toss. Heap in bowl and sprinkle remaining chips on top. Serves 6.

MAIN DISHES

BURGER BUNDLES

1 C. herb-seasoned stuffing mix
1½ lb. ground beef
⅓ C. evaporated milk
½ tsp. salt
1 can mushroom soup
1½ tsp. Worcestershire sauce
1 T. catsup
2½ T. oleo
⅓ C. water

Prepare stuffing mix according to package directions. Mix ground beef with milk. Divide into 5 or 6 patties. On waxed paper, flatten each patty to form 6" circle. Spoon ¼ C. stuffing in center of each. Draw edges over stuffing and seal. Place in 1½ quart casserole. Combine remaining ingredients and heat until bubbly. Pour over meat. Bake uncovered at 350° for 45-50 minutes. For variety, try cream of chicken or celery soup.

DANISH MEATBALLS

2 lb. ground beef
½ tsp. ginger
1 tsp. allspice
2 T. flour
1 tsp. dry mustard
2 cans cream of celery or cream of mushroom soup

Mix all of above, except soup and form into small balls. Brown in hot fat. Place in casserole. Pour soup over meatballs. Bake at 375° for 1 hour.

SPAGHETTI AND MEATBALLS

SAUCE:
1½ C. chopped onion	2 T. sugar
2 cloves, garlic, minced	1 tsp. salt
⅓ C. oil	½ tsp. pepper
8 C. tomatoes	1 T. crushed oregano
4 6-oz. cans tomato paste (2⅔ C.)	2 bay leaves
2 C. water	

MEATBALLS:
2 lb. ground beef	2 cloves garlic, minced
4 eggs	1 tsp. crushed oregano
1 C. grated Parmesan cheese	2 tsp. salt & dash pepper
¼ C. chopped parsley	

Mix ground beef, eggs, Parmesan cheese, parsley, garlic, oregano, salt and pepper and form into small balls, (approx. 40). Brown in oil. Cook onions and garlic in a small amount of oil until tender but not brown. Stir in next 8 ingredients of sauce recipe. Simmer uncovered, stirring occasionally for about 30 minutes. Add meatballs and cook at least another 30 minutes or longer.

SWEDISH MEATBALLS

1 lb. ground beef	½ C. milk
¾ C. bread crumbs or corn flakes	Salt & pepper, to taste
1 egg	1 can mushroom soup
1 medium onion, grated (optional)	½ C. water

Mix all ingredients except soup and water. Shape into small balls and brown. Remove balls and drain grease. Add water and soup; stir well. Add more water if needed. Return meatballs and simmer about 30 minutes.

TURKEY STRATA

4 slices white bread
2 C. diced cooked turkey
½ C. finely chopped celery
½ C. mayonnaise
Dash of pepper
½ C. chopped onion
¼ C. chopped green pepper
¾ tsp. salt
2 eggs, beaten
1½ C. milk
1 10½-oz. can cond. cream of mushroom soup
½ C. shredded sharp process American cheese

Trim crusts from 4 slices of white bread. Cube crusts. Cube 2 slices white bread. Place cubed crusts in bottom of 8 x 8 x 2-inch baking dish. Mix turkey, celery, mayonnaise, pepper, onion, green pepper and salt and spoon over bread cubes. Arrange trimmed bread slices on top of turkey mixture. Combine beaten eggs and milk and pour over all. Chill 1 hour or overnight. Stir 1 10½-oz. can of condensed cream of mushroom soup and spoon on top. Bake at 325° for about 1 hour or till set. Sprinkle cheese on top the last few minutes.

BECKETT'S MEAT LOAF

3 slices bacon
1 lb. lean ground beef
1 C. mashed crackers
2 eggs
¼ C. Worcestershire sauce
1 pkg. dry onion soup mix
½ C. chopped onion
¼ C. catsup
Salt & pepper, to taste

Mix all ingredients well and bake at 350° for about 1 hour. Add bacon to top of meat loaf.

OVEN STEAK

1-2 lbs. round steak
1 medium onion
1 T. flour
2 stalks celery
3 T. oil
1 C. water

    2 hours ahead, brown steak in oil over medium high heat in skillet. Remove meat and put in 9 x 13-inch baking dish. Add flour to skillet and brown. Slice celery and onions thinly and put in skillet. Cook until tender on medium heat. Add water, bring to a boil over high heat. Pour over meat. Cover with foil, put in 350° oven for 1¼ hours.

EASY PORK STEAKS

6 pork blade steaks
2 T. shortening
1½ tsp. salt
2 T. brown sugar
1 T. dry mustard
2 tsp. Worcestershire sauce
½ C. catsup
⅓ C. water
2 T. vinegar
4 tsp. minced onion

    Brown steaks in hot shortening on both sides. Place in baking dish. Combine remaining ingredients. Pour over steaks. Bake at 325° until fork tender.

HAM LOAF

1 lb. cured ham, ground
1 lb. lean fresh pork, ground
2 eggs

⅔ C. cracker crumbs or oatmeal
⅓ C. minute tapioca
1¼ C. milk

DRESSING:
¼ C. vinegar
½ C. water

½ C. brown sugar
1 T. prepared mustard

Mix loaf ingredients and form a loaf. Combine dressing ingredients in a small pan and boil a few minutes. Pour over loaf and bake at 350° for about 2 hours or less, baste occasionally. Dressing should become thick and syrupy.

PHEASANT DELUXE

1 large pheasant
3 eggs, beaten
4 C. broth
1 C. mushroom soup
1 onion, chopped

½ tsp. salt
½ tsp. pepper
1½ C. celery, chopped
1½ C. grated American cheese
4 C. Ritz crackers, crushed

Simmer pheasant in salted water until tender; remove bones. Cut meat into small pieces; set aside. Beat eggs; add broth and soup. Add onion, pepper, salt, celery, cheese and crackers. Add pheasant meat and place in 9 x 13-inch baking dish. Bake at 350° for 1 hour. Makes 3 to 10 servings.

EASY SAUSAGE CASSEROLE

2 16-oz. cans potatoes or
   4 C. cooked & sliced potatoes
1 4-oz. can mushrooms (drained)
⅓ C. diced celery

1 can mushroom soup
1 C. Cheddar cheese
8 oz. brown & serve sausage

Drain and slice potatoes. Combine potatoes, mushrooms, celery, soup and ½ C. shredded cheese. Spoon into buttered 1½ quart casserole. Arrange sauce on top. Sprinkle remaining shredded cheese on top. Bake at 350° for 35-40 minutes. For crisper sausage, broil 4" from heat source for 5 minutes before serving.

BAKED CHOW MEIN

3½ C. boiling water
1 C. raw rice
1 lb. ground beef, browned
½ C. celery, diced
1 C. onion, chopped

5 T. soy sauce
1 T. brown sugar
2 T. butter
1 can cream of mushroom soup

Pour water over rice and let stand. Add remaining ingredients to browned ground beef. Mix all and bake at 350° for 1 hour.

CHILI RILLENOS

1 lb. Jack cheese
3 eggs, beaten
1 small can evaporated milk (½ at a time)

1 can tomato sauce
2 small can Ortega chilies
½ to ¾ lb. Cheddar cheese

Grated cheese into 9 x 12-inch greased casserole. Beat eggs with evaporated milk and sprinkle over cheese. Scrape seeds from chilies and spread over above ingredients. Sprinkle with remaining milk. Pour tomato sauce over all. Sprinkle cheese over the top and bake at 350° for about 30 minutes. Allow to stand 10 minutes before serving.

CROCK POT CASSEROLE

2 lb. round steak
1 tsp. salt
¼ tsp. pepper
1 onion, thinly sliced
3 to 4 potatoes
1 16-oz. can green beans
1 clove garlic or garlic salt
1 14½-oz. can whole tomatoes
1 10¾-oz. can tomato soup

Cut steak into ½-inch thick pieces. Season with salt and pepper. Place in bottom of crock pot. On top of that place onions, potatoes (peeled & diced), green beans and garlic. Top with soup and tomatoes. Cover and cook on low 8 to 10 hours or on high 4 to 5 hours. Remove cover during last half half if too much liquid has collected.

HAMBURGER-CORN CASSEROLE

1½ lb. hamburger
1 C. chopped onion
1 12-oz. can corn (drained)
1 can cream of chicken soup
1 can cream of mushroom soup
1 C. sour cream
1¼ C. chopped pimentos
Salt
Pepper
3 C. medium cooked noodles
1 C. soft bread crumbs
3 T. melted butter

Brown hamburger, drain if too much grease. Add onion. Cook but do not brown. Add corn, soups, sour cream, pimentos, salt and pepper to taste; mix well. Stir in noodles. Pour into 2 quart casserole. Mix bread crumbs and butter. Sprinkle over top. Bake at 350° for 30 minutes. Serves 8 to 10 people.

LASAGNE

1 lb. ground beef
2 T. chopped parsley
¼ tsp. garlic powder
3 cans (8 oz.) tomato sauce
1 lb. sliced mozzarella cheese

1 pt. lard curd cottage cheese
2 T instant minced onion
¼ C. chopped celery
1½ tsp. salt
1 pkg. lasagne noodles

In a large skillet, brown ground beef. Stir in onion, parsley, celery, garlic powder, salt and tomato sauce. Cover and simmer 15 minutes. Cook noodles as directed on package. Rinse under cold water and drain. In 13 x 9 x 12-inch oiled pan or dish, layer ⅓ each of the noodles, mozzarella, cottage cheese and meat sauce. Repeat layers twice ending with meat sauce. Bake at 350° for about 30 minutes. This is a mild lasagne - for a spicier taste, sprinkle with Parmesan cheese before serving.

ONION PIE

1¼ C. soda cracker crumbs
⅓ C. melted butter
2 C. thinly sliced onion
1½ C. grated Cheddar cheese

2 eggs
½ tsp. salt
½ tsp. pepper
1 C. scalded milk

Fry onions in butter until soft and lightly brown. Mix crumbs and ⅓ C. melted butter. Press on bottom and sides of 9'' pie plate. Layer onions over bottom. Place cheese on top of onions. Beat eggs slightly and add salt and pepper; add milk. Dribble this over the pie. Bake at 325° for 50 minutes. (Pie may be baked 25 minutes one day then returned to oven for final cooking next day.) Good cold as well as hot!

DESSERTS

FRESH PEACH OR STRAWBERRY ICE CREAM

PEACH ICE CREAM:
6 to 8 fresh peaches
4 eggs
2 to 2½ C. sugar
1 to 2 C. whipping cream
1½ tsp. vanilla
Milk to fill freezer can

STRAWBERRY ICE CREAM:
3 pt. strawberries (sub. for peaches)
3 to 3¼ C. sugar

Beat eggs; add sugar and some milk. Mix well. Pour into freezer can and add cream and vanilla. Peel peaches, mash or puree in blender. Combine with a mixture in freezer can. Add enough milk to fill can. Stir to blend all ingredients together and freezer.

For strawberry ice cream substitute 3 pints of strawberries for peaches and increase sugar.

RUM SAUCE

1 C. sugar
2 T. flour
2 C. boiling water
1 T. butter
2 T. rum flavoring

Mix sugar and flour together; gradually add boiling water. Cook until mixture becomes thick. Add butter and rum flavoring. Stir to blend. You may use vanilla, lemon or other flavorings. This is good on hot mincemeat pie or apple pie.

NEVER FAIL CHOCOLATE SAUCE

1 13-oz. can evaporated milk
2 C. sugar
1 tsp. vanilla
3 sq. unsweetened chocolate

Combine all ingredients except vanilla and bring to a boil, stirring constantly. Boil 5 minutes. Remove from heat and stir in vanilla. Beat with egg beater for 1 minute. Makes 1 pint.

BUTTERMILK ICE CREAM

Yield: 1 gallon (use a 1½ gallon freezer):
4 qt. buttermilk
7 C. sugar
⅓ C. lemon rind
1¾ C. lemon juice (10-12 lemons)

Yield: 1 quart (use 2 quart freezer):
1 qt. buttermilk
1¾ C. sugar
½ C. lemon rind
½ C. lemon juice (2-3 lemons)

Combine all ingredients; stir to blend and dissolve sugar. When sugar is dissolved, pour mixture into freezer can. Place can in freezing tub, attach parts and start motor. Fill around can with ice and salt. Freeze until stiff.

STRAWBERRY CHIFFON SQUARES

⅓ C. oleo
1 3-oz. pkg. strawberry Jello
¾ C. boiling water
1 10-oz. pkg. frozen sliced strawberries
 (in syrup & thawed)
1½ C. graham crackers (crush fine)
1 can Eagle Brand milk (14 oz.)
2 C. miniature marshmallows
1 C. cream, whipped or Cool Whip
Fresh strawberries to garnish (opt.)

In small pan melt oleo. Stir in crumbs and pat firmly on the bottom of an 11 x 7 inch baking dish. Chill. In large bowl dissolve Jello in boiling water. Stir in Eagle Brand milk and undrained strawberries. Fold in marshmallows and whipped cream. Pour on crust. Chill until set. Garnish with Cool Whip and fresh strawberries. (Rather than garnish each piece, I usually spread the Cool Whip on top of the whole dessert and if I don't have fresh strawberries, I sprinkle chopped nuts on the Cool Whip, chill and then cut into squares.)

PUMPKIN ICE CREAM SQUARES (Serves 9)

1½ C. graham cracker crumbs
¼ C. melted butter
½ C. brown sugar
1 tsp. cinnamon
¼ tsp. cloves
¼ C. sugar
1 can (16 oz.) pumpkin
½ tsp. salt
¼ tsp. ginger
1 qt. softened vanilla ice cream

Whipped cream & pecans (optional)

Mix crumbs with sugar and butter. Press into 9" square pan. Combine pumpkin with sugar, salt and spices. Fold in ice cream. Pour into crumb lined pan. Cover, freezer until firm. Cut into squares about 20 minutes before serving. Top with whipped cream and nuts.

SEX DRIVE

Now, be honest. What would your MOTHER
say if she knew you up and turned to this section first?

APPETIZERS & BEVERAGES

DILLY DIP

1 C. Hellman's mayonnaise
1 C. sour cream
1½ tsp. beau monde
1½ tsp. dill weed
1½ tsp. onion powder
Fresh ground pepper
   Mix all together.

DILL DIP

1 C. mayonnaise
1 C. sour cream
1 tsp. Beau Monde (seasoning)
2 T. dill
1 tsp. onion
   Mix all together and refrigerate. Good vegetable dip.

VEGETABLE DIP

2 eggs
2 T. vinegar
2 T. sugar
8 oz. pkg. cream cheese
1 sm. jar pimento (well drained)
Chopped onions
   Cook eggs, vinegar and sugar slowly until thick. Cool slightly, then put in blender and add rest of ingredients. Blend well.

DILLIES WITH RAW VEGETABLES

Any amount of hamburger   Sliced tomatoes
Sliced carrots   Sliced cukes
Sliced potatoes   Sliced cheese
Sliced onions   1-2 cans mushroom soup

Put hamburger on bottom of pan. Layer with each of the vegetables. Spread mushroom soup. Bake at 450° for 1 hour.

FIRESIDE COFFEE

1 C. instant coffee   1½ C. sugar
2 C. non-dairy creamer   1 tsp. cinnamon
2 C. instant cocoa mix   ½ tsp. nutmeg

Mix all ingredients. Use 3 or 4 tsp. in mug of hot water.

SLUSH

½ gallon fruit sherbet
2 qt. gingerale or white soda
⅓ of 46 oz. can unsweetened pineapple juice

NOEL NIBBLERS

1 sm. jar peach jam
1 (20 oz.) can pineapple tidbits or chunks
4 C. barbeque sauce
1 lb. ground chuck
1 pkg. hot dogs

Simmer the jam and B-B-Q sauce with (optional spices) for 20 minutes. Make ground chuck into walnut size meatballs and cut hot dogs into 1-inch slices, add to sauce, also the pineapple. Heat thoroughly and serve hot. Optional Spices: Salt, pepper, onion salt or flakes and meat seasoning.

GREEN PEPPER SPREAD

5 T. butter
4 to 5 eggs (beaten)
5 T. vinegar
5 T. sugar
¾ tsp. salt
14 oz. cream cheese
10 T. green pepper
3 T. onions

Melt butter; add eggs, vinegar, salt and sugar. Stir constantly until thickened. Remove from heat. Stir in cream cheese until melted. Add peppers and onions. Refrigerate at least 4 hours before serving.

OYSTER SNACK CRACKERS

1 pkg. oyster crackers
1 sm. pkg. Hidden Valley Ranch
   Dressing (originial)
½ tsp. lemon pepper
1 tsp. dill weed
½ C. vegetable oil

Place crackers in tupperware bowl, sprinkle mixed seasonings over them. Warm oil and drizzle over cracker mixture. Shake or stir gently. Cover and let set for at least 1 hour before serving.

DIP

1 sm. carton cottage cheese
1 sm. carton sour cream
1 pkg. Hidden Valley seasoning
1 C. Hellman's mayonnaise

   Mix well and refrigerate.

VEGETABLE DIP

1 C. real mayonnaise
2 tsp. soy sauce
½ tsp. ginger
2 T. minced onion
1 tsp. vinegar
2 T. milk

Mix first five ingredients together, then add milk. Refrigerate. Serve with carrot and celery sticks, green peppers, cauliflower, etc.

CANDY & COOKIES

BROWNIES

2 C. sugar
½ C. cocoa
1¼ C. melted margarine or
   1¼ C. liquid shortening
5 eggs

2 tsp. vanilla
1½ C. flour
1 tsp. salt
½-1 C. chopped nuts
Marshamllows, if desired

    Mix sugar and cocoa together. Stir in shortening. Add eggs, 1 at a time, beating well after each. Add flour, vanilla, salt and nuts. Bake in greased and floured 9 x 13-inch pan at 350° for 18-20 minutes or until done. Take from the oven and cover with miniature marshmallows. Return to oven just long enough for the marshmallows to puff. Do not brown.

FROSTING #1:
5 T. butter
6 T. milk

1½ C. sugar
¾ C. chocolate chips

    Bring butter, milk and sugar to rolling boil. Boil 30 seconds. Add ¾ C. chocolate chips and beat until right to spread on brownies.

FROSTING #2:
1 C. sugar
⅓ C. milk
3 T. cocoa

¼ C. butter
Dash salt
Powdered sugar

    Boil sugar, milk, cocoa, butter and salt together for 1 minute. Cool and add powdered sugar to right spreading consistency. Mix well and spread on cooled brownies.

RICE KRISPIES COOKIES

½ C. peanut butter
1 6-oz. or 10-oz. pkg. butterscotch chips

3 C. Rice Krispies

    Put peanut butter and chips in double boiler and stir until completely melted and smooth. Add Rice Krispies to first mixture and stir until well mixed. Pour into an 8 x 8-inch buttered pan. Smooth with a buttered spatula or your hands. Let stand until well set and then cut into squares.

MARSHMALLOW TREATS

¼ C. margarine
4 C. miniature marshmallows
5 C. Rice Krispies

Melt margarine in large saucepan over low heat. Add marshmallow and stir until completely melted. Cook over low heat 3 minutes longer, stirring constantly. Add Rice Krispies. Stir until well coated. Using buttered spatula, press mixture evenly into buttered 13 x 9-inch pan. Cut into squares when cool. Makes 24 squares, 2 x 2 inch.

CARAMEL-FUDGE BROWNIES

½ C. melted butter
½ C. melted oleo
¼ C. cocoa
4 eggs
2 C. sugar
1½ C. sifted flour
2 tsp. vanilla
½ tsp. salt
½ C. chopped nuts
Marshmallows

Blend cocoa in with the melted butter and oleo. In mixing bowl, beat eggs; add sugar and butter-cocoa mixture. Beat and add flour, vanilla, salt and nuts; blend. Bake in greased 9 x 13-inch pan in 350° oven for 30 minutes. Cover most of the top of brownies with miniature marshmallows. Return to oven for 2 or 3 minutes. When cool, frost with caramel icing.

CARAMEL ICING:

½ C. butter or oleo
1 C. brown sugar, packed
4 T. milk
2 C. powdered sugar (sifted)

Boil butter and brown sugar over medium heat for 2 minutes. Add milk and bring back to boil. As soon as it reaches the boil stage, remove from heat. Add sifted powdered sugar. Stir until thick. Spread on top of cooled brownies.

PEANUT BUTTER CRUNCHIES

¾ C. light corn syrup
¾ C. firmly packed brown sugar
¾ C. peanut butter
6 C. Rice Krispies

Combine syrup and sugar. Cook over medium heat until mixture bubbles. Remove from heat. Add peanut butter. Stir until well combined. Spread in greased pan.

BREADS

PUFF BALL DOUGHNUTS

3 eggs
1½ C. sugar
1 pt. milk
2 tsp. baking powder
1 tsp. vanilla
4-5 C. flour

Mix in order given. Make stiff enough so spoon will stand upright. Drop by teaspoonful into hot oil or fat in deep fat fryer. Roll in sugar as you take them out of fat, or shake in a sack with sugar.

MONKEY BREAD

3 cans buttermilk biscuits
½ tsp. cinnamon
¾ C. sugar
½ C. sugar
1 stick oleo
¾ tsp. cinnamon

OR

¾ C. sugar
4 tubes of biscuits
¾ C. oleo
1 tsp. cinnamon
1 C. sugar
1½ tsp. cinnamon

Cut biscuits in quarters and roll in mixture of ½ cup sugar and ½ tsp. cinnamon or put ¾ cup sugar and 1 tsp. cinnamon in paper bag, drop quartered biscuits into sugar mixture and shake. Drop coated pieces in greased and floured bundt or tube pan. Bring to boil the sugar, oleo and cinnamon. Pour over biscuit pieces and bake 30-45 minutes at 350°. Cool 5-10 minutes and invert onto serving plate.

OATMEAL MUFFINS

1½ C. dry oatmeal
1 C. hot milk
4 T. shortening
½ C. sugar
¾ C. flour
4 tsp. baking powder
¼ tsp. salt

Add oatmeal to hot milk; cool. Let stand 10 minutes. Add rest of ingredients and mix well. Bake at 400° for 20 minutes.

WAFFLES

4 heaping T. flour
Pinch of salt
Milk
2 eggs
2 tsp. baking powder
Pinch of soda
1 heaping T. lard

Combine flour, baking powder, salt and soda. Add enough milk to make like pancakes. Add melted lard. Add beaten egg yolks and mix. Fold in well beaten (stiff) egg whites last.

CORN BREAD

1½ C. flour
2 T. sugar
1¼ tsp. salt
⅔ C. corn meal
3 tsp. baking powder
1 egg
⅔ C. sweet milk
½ C. shortening

Sift dry ingredients together. Mix liquids and turn into dry ingredients and stir until all the flour is dampened. Don't over stir. Bake in greased muffin pans in hot oven.

CINNAMON ROLLS

1 C. warm water	2 T. evaporated milk
1¼ C. sugar	½ tsp. salt
¼ C. melted margarine	1 yeast cake
2 eggs, beaten	4½ C. flour
2 tsp. cinnamon	⅓ C. raisins (optional)

Combine water, milk, ½ cup sugar, salt, margarine and yeast. Stir until dissolved; add eggs and half of flour. Beat until smooth. Stir in remaining flour to make slightly stiff dough. Knead on lightly floured board until smooth and elastic. Place in greased bowl, cover and let rise 1 hour. Punch down; turn on lightly floured board and divide in half. Roll each half to a 11-inch square. Spread with 3 T. butter. Roll up as for jelly roll; seal edges firmly and make 12 slices. Place cut side up in greased 9 x 13-inch or 9 x 15-inch pan and cover. Let rise 30 minutes. Bake at 350° for 25-30 minutes. Glaze when cool with mixture of 1½ C. powdered sugar, 2 T. margarine, 1¼ tsp. vanilla and 1-2 T. hot water.

BEST PIZZA CRUST

1 pkg. yeast	¾ C. warm water
½ tsp. salt	½ tsp. sugar
1 tsp. oil	

Dissolve yeast and sugar in warm water and add salt, oil and enough flour to make a stiff dough. Let rise 10 minutes. Press onto 2 pizza pans. I sprinkle with butter-flavored salt and let raise 10 more minutes. Add favorite toppings.

NOODLES

1 C. flour	1 tsp. baking powder
½ tsp. salt	1 tsp. melted butter
1 egg	2 T. milk

Mix flour, baking powder and salt. Make a well in center and place egg, melted butter and milk in it. Mix well. Let rest 20 minutes. Roll out and either cut right away or dry first.

BUTTERMILK BISCUITS

2 C. flour	3 tsp. baking powder
¼ tsp. soda	4 T. Crisco
1 tsp. salt	1 C. buttermilk

Mix as for biscuits. Coat with buttermilk before baking. Bake in 425° for 12-15 minutes. Makes 14 biscuits.

GRAHAM GEMS

2 eggs	½ C. sugar
½ tsp. salt	¾ tsp. soda
1 tsp. baking powder	1 C. sour cream
3¾ C. graham flour	1½ C. milk

Combine as for muffins. Bake in muffin tins at 350° until done.

VEGGIES

VEGETABLE CASSEROLE

1 (10 oz.) pkg. frozen cauliflower
1 (10 oz.) pkg. frozen lima beans
1 (10 oz.) pkg. frozen broccoli
1 can mushroom soup
1 (8 oz.) container sour cream

Mix all ingredients together, place in casserole dish and top with grated cheese.

CORN CASSEROLE (Serves 10)

1 can whole kernel corn (drained)
1 can cream style corn
8 oz. sour cream
1 egg (2 is better)
1 small onion (chopped)
Salt & pepper, to taste
Dried parsley
1 pkg. Jiffy corn muffin mix

Combine all ingredients and stir together. Bake for 45 minutes at 350°.

VEGETABLES IN CHEESE SAUCE

2 pkgs. frozen broccoli & cauliflower
  (cooked & drained)
¼ C. milk
1 can cond. cheddar cheese soup
¼ C. buttered bread crumbs

Place broccoli and cauliflower in shallow baking dish. Blend soup and milk; pour over broccoli and cauliflower. Top with crumbs. Bake in a 350° oven, about 30 minutes or until hot and bubbling. Makes 6 to 8 servings.

CHEESE CARROTS

10-12 carrots (sliced)
¼ C. butter
1 medium onion (chopped)
¼ C. flour
1 tsp. salt
¼ tsp. dry mustard
2 C. milk
Pepper, to taste
¼ tsp. celery salt
½ lb. Velveeta cheese
Buttered bread crumbs

Cook carrots. Melt butter; add flour, mustard, milk and seasonings. Place carrots in casserole. Add onions and cheese sauce. Put in casserole and top with bread crumbs. Bake at 350° for 25 minutes.

OVEN-BROWNED POTATO WEDGES

4 medium-sized baking potatoes
4 T. melted butter
Salt

Peel potatoes, cut in half lengthwise and then each half in thirds lengthwise. (Each potato yields size pieces.) Blanch wedges in boiling, unsalted water for 3 minutes. Drain and pat dry with paper towels. Arrange potato wedges in single layer in greased baking dish. Dribble melted butter over tops and salt potatoes. Bake at 450° for 15 minutes. Turn potatoes, and salt again. Bake another 15 minutes.

POT LUCK SWEET POTATOES

17 oz. can sweet potatoes
2 T. brown sugar
1½ T. cornstarch
¼ tsp. salt
½ tsp. cinnamon

1 C. apricot juice
16 oz. can apricot halves
2 T. butter
½ C. pears

Place sliced potatoes halves in baking dish. In saucepan, combine sugar, cornstarch, salt, cinnamon and apricot juice. Boil for 2 minutes; add butter and apricots. Pour syrup over sweet potatoes. Sprinkle on nuts and bake at 350° for 25 minutes.

POTATOES BYRON

6 large baking potatoes
½ lb. butter (melted)
½ tsp. salt
Pepper, to taste

¼ C. grated onion
½ C. Half & Half
¾ C. coarsley grated longhorn cheese

Bake potatoes, cut and slice off each potato and scoop out pulp, (do not mash, but break up coarsley). Add butter, salt, pepper and onions. Turn into a 9-inch glass pie pan, pour cream over and let stand for 30 minutes. Sprinkle with cheese and bake in pre-heated 375° oven for 20 to 30 minutes or until cheese melts and forms a golden crust. Serves 6. (If potatoes are smaller, cut down on the amount of butter. The potatoes should not be mushy.)

BUFFET POTATO CASSEROLE

2 lb. pkg. hash browns
½ C. butter (melted)
1 pt. dairy sour cream
1 can cream of chicken soup
½ C. chopped onion
1 tsp. salt
2 C. shredded Cheddar cheese or Cheddar soup
½ tsp. pepper
2 C. corn flakes, crumbled
½ C. butter (melted)

Combine potatoes and ½ C. melted butter in a large bowl. Stir in sour cream, soup, onion, cheese, salt and pepper. Place in greased 9 x 13-inch pan. Sprinkle over top, cover with foil and bake 20 minutes. Uncover and continue baking 20 minutes. Makes 12 servings. *Note: This casserole can be made in advance and refrigerated. If so add 10 minutes to baking time.

SCALLOPED POTATOES

6 large potatoes
1 can of celery soup
½ C. milk

Peel and slice the potatoes. Pour the soup over the potatoes. Also the milk. Stir together and bake at 350° for 50 minutes.

SOUPS & SANDWICHES

SOUTH OF THE BORDER CHILI
Diane Neely

1 lb. ground beef
1 C. chopped onion
2 medium cloves of garlic (minced)
2 cans tomato soup
2 cans (15 oz. ea.) kidney beans
3 C. cooked macaroni
½ C. water
2 T. vinegar
3 T. chili powder
Salt & pepper, to taste

In a large saucepan, brown beef, cook onion and garlic. Stir to separate meat. Add remaining ingredients and simmer 30 minutes. Stir occasionally. Garnish with parsley if desired.

MATT'S CHILI
Mrs. Matt J. Schulte

1 lb. ground beef
1 onion (chopped)
2 T. flour
1 large can chili beans
1 large can tomato juice
1 C. water
1 T. chili powder

Brown beef and onion, then add flour. Add remaining ingredients and several hours simmer or put in a crock pot on low.

BEEF STEW

2 lb. beef stew meat
1 pkg. dry onion soup mix
1 can cream of mushroom soup
1 can water

Mix water with both soups. Pour over uncooked meat in large roaster or casserole. Cover and cook at 300° for three hours without opening. Add cubed potatoes and another vegetable or two 1 hour before serving. This makes a dark brown flavorful stew.

BARBECUED BEEF FOR 20 BUNS

4 lb. pot roast

Cook until tender, cool, remove fat and shred meat. Put meat with broth and combine with:

1 can tomato soup	2 T. brown sugar
1 bottle catsup	½ tsp. dry mustard
1 C. water	1 medium onion (chopped)
2 T. lemon juice	Celery, bay leaf and salt and pepper
2 T. Worcestershire sauce	to taste

Simmer about 1½ hours. Serve on buns. Freezes well.

BARBECUED BEEFBURGERS

1 lb. hamburger	¼ C. catsup
½ C. onions (chopped)	1 tsp. salt
¼ C. celery (chopped)	½ tsp. pepper
¼ C. green pepper (chopped)	1 tsp. vinegar
1-6 oz. can tomato sauce	1½ tsp. Worcestershire sauce
	1 T. sugar

Brown onions, celery and green pepper in small amount of shortening. Add hamburger and brown lightly. Add other ingredients and simmer until thick. Serve on buns.

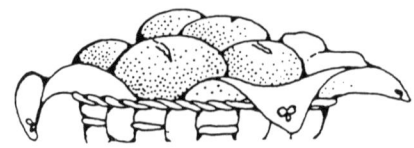

PINWHEEL SANDWICHES

4 C. flour	1 tsp. salt
2 T. baking powder	2 T. sugar

Mix and add 1 C. shortening and 1½ C. milk. Roll out dough to two 12x14-inch oblongs. Mix 1½ lbs. lean sausage that's been browned with 1 can finely chopped Spam. Spread meat mixture on dough. Roll like jelly roll. Cut into 1 to 1⅓-inch sections and put on cookie sheets. Bake at 400° until brown.

SALADS

MAMA'S APPLE SALAD

1 large delicious apple	¼ C. vinegar
1 large banana	1 egg or 2 yolks
Drained pineapple (optional)	1 tsp. salt
English walnuts (optional)	¾ C. sugar
1 rounded T. margarine	3 heaping T. flour
1 C. Carnation evaporated milk	1 tsp. vanilla

Prepare salad dressing first. Measure vinegar into cup and fill with water. Heat to a boil; set aside. Mix together in a 3 or 4 cup pan, egg, salt, sugar and flour. Add a little of the vinegar water and mix, then add the remainder of the vinegar water and the margarine and cook until thick. Remove from stove and add the milk and vanilla; cool. This makes about a pint.

For Salad: Peel and cut apple into pieces and slice banana. Into bowl add enough dressing to coat. Drained pineapple and English walnuts may be added if desired. Serves about 4. (May be served on lettuce.)

SUPER SALAD

1 lb. macaroni	1 C. sugar
1 large green pepper (chopped)	1 C. vinegar
4 carrots (shredded)	2 C. mayonnaise
1 onion (chopped)	1 tsp. salt
1 can sweetened cond. milk	¼ tsp. pepper

Cook macaroni; drain and cool. Add remaining ingredients. Mix thoroughly. Chill at least for 4 hours. Store in a plastic container.

MACARONI SALAD

3 C. cooked macaroni
1½ C. ham or bologna (cubed)
1 C. cubed cheese
½ C. chopped celery
Salt
Mustard

¼ C. chopped onion
3 diced hard boiled eggs
¾ C. chopped sweet pickles
Salad dressing
Pepper

Stir salad dressing into macaroni, ham, cheese, celery, onion, eggs and pickles with a little mustard, salt and pepper, to taste.

RED CABBAGE

1 medium head cabbage
1 rounded T. shortening
½ C. vinegar or lemon juice

1 tsp. salt
¼ C. sugar
¼ C. currant jelly (optional)

Melt shortening in a sufficiently large kettle, add cabbage and vinegar (sweet pickle vinegar may be used), salt and sugar. Cook gently until tender, then season to taste with additional salt, sugar and vinegar. Beet pickle juice is often used instead of vinegar. Add jelly instead of last sugar. Red cabbage is a popular dish at Christmas time.

QUICK SUMMER SALAD

1 head of cauliflower
¼ C. chopped onion
10 oz. pkg. frozen peas
1 C. sharp Cheddar cheese (shred)
1 pkg. Good Seasons buttermilk farm style salad dressing mix

Prepare dressing mix according to package directions; set aside. Cut cauliflower into bite-size pieces. Mix in onions, peas and cheese. Pour salad dressing over all and stir. Refrigerate for 2 to 3 hours before serving.

SAUERKRAUT SALAD

1 large can sauerkraut (wash & drain well)
½ C. oil
½ C. vinegar
1 C. sugar (½ C. sugar & ½ C. artifical sweetner)

Mix well and let marinate overnight. Can use onion, pimento, and celery if you like.

COPPER PENNY SALAD

2 lbs. carrots (sliced)
1 small green pepper
1 onion
1 can tomato soup
½ C. salad oil
1 C. sugar
¾ C. vinegar
1 tsp. mustard
1 tsp. Worcestershire sauce
Salt
Pepper

Cook carrots till tender, but not mushy. Mix dressing adding chopped onion and pepper. Pour over cooled carrots and refrigerate.

CINNAMON APPLESAUCE REVEL SALAD

2 pkgs. (3 ozs. ea.) lemon or cherry gelatin
⅓ C. red cinnamon candies
2½ C. boiling water
2 C. applesauce
1 T. lemon juice
Dash of salt
½ to 1 tsp. red food coloring

Stirring constantly, dissolve candies in boiling water while still on stove. Remove from heat and dissolve gelatin in water, then add lemon juice and food coloring and salt. Cool until thickened and fold in applesauce. Chill until firm.

BLUEBERRY SALAD

2 small boxes black raspberry gelatin
1 can blueberry pie filling
2 C. boiling water
1 large can crushed pineapple
1 (9 oz.) carton Cool Whip

Dissolve gelatin in boiling water; add pineapple juice. Reserve ¾ cup and let hot mixture set. Add pineapple and pie filling to large mixture. Whip the ¾ cup gelatin with Cool Whip. Spread on fruit layer.

CHERRY SALAD

1 can cherry pie filling
1 small can chunk pineapple
2 bananas (sliced)
1 C. miniature marshmallows

Late afternoon mix cherry pie filling and pineapple (cut smaller). Let sit in refrigerator overnight. Add bananas and marshmallows. Mix well and serve.

COTTAGE CHEESE SALAD

1 (16 oz.) carton cottage cheese
1 can crushed pineapple
1 C. miniature marshmallows
1 pt. Cool Whip
1 (3 oz.) box strawberry or cherry Jello (dry)

Mix all together for quick easy salad.

APPLESAUCE JELLO SALAD

¼ C. cinnamon candies
2 C. boiling water
1 large box cherry gelatin
2 C. applesauce

Dissolve candies in water. Add gelatin. Cool and add applesauce. Chill till firm.

SHRIMP SALAD

8 oz. pkg. frozen shrimp (not breaded)
1 C. carrots
1 C. onions
1 C. celery
Shoestring potatoes
Mayonnaise

Mix all with mayonnaise. Before serving - add shoestring potatoes.

MACARONI SALAD

1 lb. macaroni
1 large green pepper (chopped)
1 medium onion (chopped)
½-1 C. vinegar
1 tsp. salt
1 C. diced celery (optional)

4 shredded carrots
1 C. sugar
1 can Eagle Brand milk
2 C. mayonnaise
¼ tsp. pepper
1 C. crushed pineapple (optional)

Cook macaroni and drain, then mix with all other ingredients. Store in tight container and refrigerate at least 4 hours before using.

FRUIT FILLED MACARONI SALAD

1 (8¼ oz.) can crushed pineapple
4 beaten eggs
½ C. sugar
¼ C. lemon juice
1 pkg. Dream Whip

3 C. cooked ring macaroni
(1½ C. uncooked)
3 C. diced apples
1 C. mini-marshmallows

Drain pineapple (save juice) and chill pineapple. Combine egg, syrup, sugar and lemon juice. Cook and stir over heat till mixture thickens; add macaroni. Cover and chill for a few hours. Whip cream and fold into macaroni along with apple, marshmallows and pineapple. Cool Whip can be used in place of Dream Whip.

CAULIFLOWER SALAD

1 head of cauliflower
1 (10 oz.) pkg. frozen peas
½ C. or less chopped onion
1 C. celery (chopped)

DRESSING:
1½ tsp. dry Hidden Valley original salad dressing
¼ C. milk
1 C. mayonnaise
Mix and pour dressing over all. Better if made at least 12 hours ahead. Keeps several days.

COLE SLAW

1 T. Knox gelatin
¼ C. cold water
1 C. vinegar
1½ C. sugar
1 tsp. salt
1 C. oil
¼ tsp. pepper
8 C. shredded cabbage
2 green peppers (diced)
2 carrots (shredded)
1½ medium onions (chopped)

Dissolve gelatin and water; set aside. Boil vinegar, sugar and salt. Mix with gelatin; cool, when it turns creamy add oil and pepper. Cool dressing and toss with cabbage, green peppers, carrots and onion. Keeps very well.

GOOD CABBAGE SALAD

1 head of cabbage (shredded)
1 chopped onion
Any amount of green pepper
Small jar of green stuffed olives
1 C. sugar

Pour the sugar over the other ingredients and let stand. (May add grated carrots sometimes.)

DRESSING:
1 C. vinegar
½ C. salad oil
1 tsp. salt
1 tsp. pepper
1 tsp. prepared mustard
1 tsp. Worcestershire sauce
1 tsp. celery seed

Boil ingredients together for 3 minutes. Pour over cabbage mixture and let cool before using. Will keep several weeks in refrigerator.

WARM WEATHER SALAD

Raw cauliflower
Broccoli
Onion
1 cucumber
Cherry tomatoes
Hidden Valley Ranch dressing

    Mix Hidden Valley Ranch dressing. Pour over all and marinate for at least 2 hours. This keeps well and can be made ahead of time.

HOT AND HEARTY POTATO SALAD

1 C. chopped onions
1 T. margarine
½ C. Hellman's real mayonnaise
⅓ C. cider vinegar
1 T. sugar
1¾ tsp. salt
¼ tsp. pepper
4 medium potatoes (cooked, peeled & sliced (about 4 C.)
1 T. chopped parsley
4 T. cooked & crumbled bacon

    In a large skillet over medium heat, cook onions in margarine for 2 to 3 minutes. Stir in next 5 ingredients. Add potatoes and continue cooking, stirring constantly, about 2 minutes or until heated through (do not boil). Garnish with parsley and bacon. Serves 6.

APPLE SALAD

6 apples (chopped)
2 sticks celery (cut-up)
½ C. chopped walnuts
1 C. miniature marshmallows
1½ tsp. lemon juice
3 T. or more salad dressing

    Mix well, chill and serve.

MAIN DISHES

BEEF CASSEROLE

2 lb. ground beef
½ tsp. salt
¼ tsp. pepper
8 potatoes (thinly sliced)
1 onion, chopped
1 can 20¾-oz. pork & beans
2 cans 10¾-oz. tomato soup

Combine meat, salt and pepper. Place potatoes in bottom of casserole. Top with onion. Cover with beef, pork and beans and soup. Cover and bake 1½ hours at 375°.

ALICE'S EGGS (6 Servings)

1 C. grated cheese
2 T. butter
½ C. half & half (or Carnation milk)
½ tsp. salt
1/8 tsp. pepper
1 tsp. dry mustard
8 eggs

Grease an 8 x 8-inch pan. Grate cheese on bottom of pan, dot with butter. Mix half and half, salt, pepper and mustard. Pour half of this over cheese. Beat eggs slightly, add rest of half & half mixture. Pour over cheese. May add ham pieces or crumbled bacon. Bake at 325° for 40 minutes. Cut in squares to serve.

CHOP SUEY

2 T. fat
1 lb. ground beef
1 C. sliced onions
2 C. sliced celery
1 C. rice
1½ C. tomato juice
1 tsp. salt

Brown beef in fat. Add remaining ingredients and simmer on low heat.

TERIYAKI STEAK

1 lb. round steak
1/8 tsp. garlic powder
½ tsp. onion powder
2 T. sugar
¼ C. soy sauce
¼ C. water
½ tsp. meat tenderizer

    Mix spices, sugar and meat tenderizer, soy sauce and water till dissolved. Pour over steak. Refrigerate for 24 hours, turning once. Broil to desired doneness, or grill.

GERMAN SAUERBRATEN

4 lb. boneless beef roast
2 C. wine vinegar
2 C. water
2 onions (peeled & sliced)
3 bay leaves
½ tsp. pepper
6 whole cloves
2 T. sugar
¼ C. fat

    Place beef roast in a large bowl. Combine remaining ingredients, except fat and bring to a boil. Pour over meat and cover. Place meat in refrigerator for two or three days. Turn several times. Remove meat and save marinade. Dry meat off with paper towel. Heat fat and brown meat on all sides, strain marinade. Add 1 C. and some onions to the meat. Cover and cook for 1 hour and a half at 350°. Half way through, add one pkg. of brown gravy mix to remaining marinade and add to meat.

PORK CHOPS IN THE OVEN

4 to 6 lean pork chops
1 can green beans (or 1 pt. canned)
3 to 4 potatoes, sliced
3 slices bacon (cut up, but not cooked)
1 T. chopped onion
½ tsp. salt
¼ tsp. pepper

Brown pork chops in shortening in skillet. Line a casserole dish or a 9 x 13-inch pan with aluminum foil. Place the browned pork chops in the bottom and add potatoes, salt and pepper. Cover with green beans, onions and bacon. Tightly fold foil over top and seal well. Bake for 1½ to 2 hours at 350°.

BAKED PINEAPPLE

1 large can sliced pineapple
2 T. cornstarch
½ C. sugar

Drain juice and mix with sugar and cornstarch. Cook together until clear. Place pineapple slices in a 9 x 9-inch baking dish. Pour the above mixture over and bake in a 350° oven about 20 or 30 minutes or just until bubbly. Very good with ham.

CHEESE BURGER CASSEROLE

1 lb. ground beef
¼ C. chopped onion
8 oz. can tomato sauce
¼ C. catsup
Pepper to taste
½ lb. sliced cheese
1 can biscuits

Brown ground beef with onion. Drain off fat. Add tomato sauce, catsup and pepper. Alternate meat and cheese in ungreased 1½ quart casserole. Put biscuits around the edge.

CHEESE AND BACON OPEN OMELET

6 eggs
1 C. milk
1 green onion, minced
½ tsp. salt

1/8 tsp. pepper
4 oz. pkg. shredded cheddar cheese
4 slices bacon, cooked & crumbled
or bacon bits

    Preheat oven to 400°. Grease 9 x 9-inch baking dish. In bowl, mix beaten eggs, milk, onion, salt and pepper until well blended. Pour mixture into pan. Sprinkle cheese and bacon evenly over top. Bake 20 minutes or until set and golden brown, makes 4 main dish servings. Serve with chunks of hot buttered bread and jam for breakfast; or with salad and toast for lunch.

QUICHE LORRAINE

Unbaked pie crust shell
White of 1 egg
½ lb. grated Gruyere cheese
1 T. flour
6 slices bacon

1 C. minced onion
3 to 4 eggs
1 to 2 C. rich milk or cream
Salt
Dash cayenne pepper

    Use your favorite 9'' pie crust shell and brush with entire surface with egg white. Prevents sogginess. Dredge grated cheese in flour, mixing well. Fry bacon slices until nicely crisp. Drain on paper toweling and cut in tiny pieces. In bacon fat saute onions until limp and distribute the onion and bacon over the bottom of the unbaked pie shell. Cover with the mixture of grated cheese and flour. Beat 3 eggs with 1 C. of rich milk (4 eggs with 2 C. for a deeper tart), salt to taste, and add a dash of cayenne pepper. Pour over the cheese. Bake in 400° oven for ten minutes, then reduce heat to 350° and bake for 1 hour, or until knife comes out clean. Serves 6 generously or 8 scantily.

FAVORITE TACOS

Tortillas
Hamburger
Salt & pepper
Onion
Chili powder
1 can chili style beans
⅓ head lettuce, cut up
1 tomato
½ C. cut-up or grated cheese
1 heaping T. mayonnaise

Fry flat tortillas just briefly to soften, then lay on paper towel. Fry hamburger with salt, pepper, onion and chili powder. Prepare individual tacos and add taco sauce on top.

CHOW MEIN

1½ lb. hamburger
1 onion, diced
1½ tsp. salt
½ C. uncooked rice
1 can cream of mushroom soup
1 can chicken gumbo soup
2 cans water
3 carrots, sliced thin
Bean sprouts
1 C. chopped celery
2 T. soy sauce

Makes a big batch. Cook slowly as it sticks easy. Can substitute can of cream of celery soup for the chopped celery. Put the bean sprouts in when nearly done. Cook 1 hour and pour over noodles. I also add water chestnuts at the very end.

LASAGNA

1 lb. ground beef
1 onion
¼ tsp. oregano
¼ tsp. sweet basil
1 T. sugar
8 oz. cottage cheese

Mozzarella cheese (slice or shred)
Lasagna noodles
Spaghetti sauce (1 lg. or 2 sm.
Ragu - use either Thick 'n Zesty
or Sausage 'n Pepper

Brown ground beef and onion. Add spaghetti sauce, oregano, basil and sugar. Simmer while noodles cook. Layer in a 9 x 13-inch pan. Noodles, sauce (using about ⅓), cottage cheese (use ½), mozzarella cheese (using ½). Repeat above, then top off with noodles and sauce. Bake at 350° uncovered for 30 minutes.

OLD SETTLERS BAKED BEANS

½ lb. bacon (cut in pieces)
1 lb. hamburger
1 onion, diced
2 T. molasses
1 can red kidney beans

1 can butter beans
½ C. brown sugar
¼ C. catsup
½ tsp. dry mustard

Brown bacon, hamburger and onion; drain. Mix, cover and bake at 350° or less for 1 to 2 hours.

SAUSAGE BAKE

1 pkg. refrigerator biscuits
1 lb. sausage (browned)
2 C. shredded mozzarella cheese

3 eggs, slightly beaten
½ tsp. salt
¼ tsp. oregano

Heat oven to 425°. Put biscuits in small greased pan. Spoon in sausage. Cover with cheese. Combine remaining ingredients and pour over cheese. Bake 20-25 minutes or until golden brown.

TEXAS HASH

1 large onion	2 lb. can or 1 qt. whole tomatoes
1 medium green pepper	1 C. uncooked rice
3 T. shortening	2 tsp. Worcestershire sauce
1 lb. ground beef	2 tsp. salt

Cook onion and green pepper in shortening until tender, but not browned. Add beef and cook. Stir in the remaining ingredients. Pour into a greased 2 quart casserole and cover. Bake at 350° for about 60 minutes. Remove cover the last 15 minutes and top with shredded Cheddar cheese, if desired.

CHEESE SALMON BAKE

1 lb. can salmon	½ lb. grated cheese
2 C. uncooked noodles	Salt
White sauce	Pepper

Mix all ingredients thoroughly and put in a loaf pan. Bake at 375° for 30 minutes.

CHICKEN AND RICE CASSEROLE

1 chicken (picked off the bone)	1 can cream of mushroom soup
1 box minute rice	Chicken broth
1 can cream of chicken soup	

Put layer of rice in buttered casserole, then add a layer of chicken, another layer of rice and another of chicken. Mix soups together with some of the chicken broth to thin. Pour over casseroles. Bake at 375° for 25 minutes.

RICE CASSEROLE

⅓ C. Parmesan cheese
1 can consomme soup
1 can onion soup
1 can cream of chicken soup
1 stick margarine
1¼ C. rice (Uncle Ben's)
Left-over chicken, turkey or beef

Dice meat and mix all ingredients. Bake at 350° for 1 hour or until rice is done. Stir after ½ hour. Do not cover.

SCALLOPED CHICKEN

1½ qt. bread cubes
1¼ tsp. sage
¾ tsp. salt
2 T. onion
2 eggs
⅔ C. celery, diced
1 chicken cooked
1 qt. broth
4 T. chicken fat (may omit)
4 T. flour

Moisten bread cubes with ¾ C. melted butter or broth. Put chicken picked from the bones and cut in pieces in bottom of 9 x 13-inch pan. Mix first 3 ingredients together to make dressing. Pat over the top of the chicken. Pour broth and fat thickened with flour over the dressing evenly. Bake 1 hour at 350°.

DESSERTS

STRAWBERRY VANILLA DESSERT

10 C. angel food cake cubes
2 C. milk
1 qt. vanilla ice cream
3 C. boiling water
2 sm. pkg. instant vanilla pudding
2 pkg. strawberry Jello (3 oz.)
2 pkg. frozen strawberries (10 oz.)

Place cake cubes in large cake pan. (9 x 13-inch isn't large enough). Combine instant pudding with milk; add ice cream. Beat at low speed until well blended. Pour over cake cubes. Lift lightly with a fork so pudding goes around the cake cubes, but do not stir. Set in refrigerator until firm. Dissolve Jello in boiling water; add frozen strawberries and stir until Jello begins to thicken. Pour over the pudding. Chill until set. Better if made day before you wish to serve it. Serve with a spoon of Cool Whip on top. Variation: Frozen raspberries and raspberry Jello can be used instead of strawberry.

FROZEN FRUIT SLUSH

2 boxes frozen strawberries
3-5 medium bananas (chopped)
1 6-oz. can frozen orange juice
1 6-oz. can frozen lemonade
1 13-oz. can crushed pineapple
2 C. sugar
2 C. water

Mix together sugar and water; cook until clear. Let cool. Pour over fruit that has been mixed with juices. Pour into muffin cups and freeze. Remove from freezer about 15 minutes before serving.

KAYE'S FAVORITE CHOCOLATE SAUCE

1 can evaporated milk
2 C. sugar
4 oz. milk chocolate chips or 4 sq. unsweetened chocolate
1 stick butter
1 tsp. vanilla

    Place all ingredients in a saucepan and bring to a boil over medium heat. Cook until all ingredients are well blended. Remove from heat and set aside for 30 minutes. Then beat until thick. (I always use the chocolate chips.)

CHOCOLATE SYRUP

¼ C. butter or oleo
¼ C. cocoa
¾ C. sugar
⅓ C. cream (may use Half & Half)
1 T. Karo syrup
1 tsp. vanilla

    Melt butter; add cocoa, sugar, cream and syrup. Bring to a boil and boil 1 minute. Add vanilla and stir.

FROZEN FRUIT CUP

1 16-oz. can frozen lemonade
1 16-oz. can frozen orange juice
1 box frozen strawberries
2 C. crushed pineapple
1 sm. jar maraschino cherries, chop
2½ C. water
1 C. sugar
Bananas

    Put all ingredients in a bowl and stir until well blended. Pour fruit mixture into Dixie cups and freeze. Fresh fruits in season may be used; such as peaches, nectarines or whatever you choose.

PINEAPPLE ICE CREAM

4 C. sugar
No. 2½ can crushed pineapple
Juice of 1 lemon
4 eggs
1 qt. cream
Milk to fill freezer can (about 2 qt.)

    Beat eggs and sugar; add pineapple and lemon juice. Beat cream into this mixture and pour into freezer can which has been chilled until a white frost appears inside. Add enough milk to fill can to correct level. About 2 quarts. Makes 1½ gallons.

Need a Gift?

For

- Shower • Birthday • Mother's Day •
- Anniversary • Christmas •

Turn Page For Order Form
(Order Now While Supply Lasts!)

TO ORDER COPIES OF
HORMONE HELPER COOKBOOK

Please send me _____ copies of Hormone Helper Cookbook at $11.95 each.

(Make checks payable to QUIXOTE PRESS.)

Name _____

Street _____

City _____ State _____ Zip Code _____

SEND ORDERS TO:

QUIXOTE PRESS
31798 K18S
Sioux City, IA 51109
1-800-571-BOOK

- -

TO ORDER COPIES OF
HORMONE HELPER COOKBOOK

Please send me _____ copies of Hormone Helper Cookbook at $11.95 each.

(Make checks payable to QUIXOTE PRESS.)

Name _____

Street _____

City _____ State _____ Zip Code _____

SEND ORDERS TO:

QUIXOTE PRESS
31798 K18S
Sioux City, IA 51109
1-800-571-BOOK

Since you have enjoyed this book, perhaps you would be interested in some of these others from QUIXOTE PRESS.

ARKANSAS BOOKS

HOW TO TALK ARKANSAS
 by Bruce Carlson .... paperback $7.95
ARKANSAS' ROADKILL COOKBOOK
 by Bruce Carlson .... paperback $7.95
REVENGE OF ROADKILL
 by Bruce Carlson .... paperback $7.95
GHOSTS OF THE OZARKS
 by Bruce Carlson .... paperback $9.95
A FIELD GUIDE TO SMALL ARKANSAS FEMALES
 by Bruce Carlson .... paperback $9.95
LET'S US GO DOWN TO THE RIVER 'N...
 by various authors .... paperback $9.95
ARKANSAS' VANISHING OUTHOUSE
 by Bruce Carlson .... paperback $9.95
TALL TALES OF THE MISSISSIPPI RIVER
 by Dan Titus .... paperback $9.95
LOST & BURIED TREASURE OF THE MISSISSIPPI RIVER
 by Netha Bell & Gary Scholl .... paperback $9.95
TALES OF HACKETT'S CREEK
 by Dan Titus .... paperback $9.95
UNSOLVED MYSTERIES OF THE MISSISSIPPI RIVER
 by Netha Bell .... paperback $9.95
101 WAYS TO USE A DEAD RIVER FLY
 by Bruce Carlson .... paperback $7.95
VACANT LOT, SCHOOL YARD & BACK ALLEY GAMES
 by various authors .... paperback $9.95
HOW TO TALK MIDWESTERN
 by Robert Thomas .... paperback $7.95
ARKANSAS COOKIN'
 by Bruce Carlson .... (3x5) paperback $5.95

DAKOTA BOOKS

HOW TO TALK DAKOTA .... paperback $7.95
Some Pretty Tame, but Kinda Funny Stories About Early
DAKOTA LADIES-OF-THE-EVENING
 by Bruce Carlson .... paperback $9.95

SOUTH DAKOTA ROADKILL COOKBOOK
 by Bruce Carlson .... paperback $7.95
REVENGE OF ROADKILL
 by Bruce Carlson .... paperback $7.95
101 WAYS TO USE A DEAD RIVER FLY
 by Bruce Carlson .... paperback $7.95
LET'S US GO DOWN TO THE RIVER 'N...
 by various authors .... paperback $9.95
LOST & BURIED TREASURE OF THE MISSOURI RIVER
 by Netha Bell .... paperback $9.95
MAKIN' DO IN SOUTH DAKOTA
 by various authors .... paperback $9.95
GUNSHOOTIN', WHISKEY DRINKIN', GIRL CHASIN' STORIES
OUT OF THE OLD DAKOTAS
 by Netha Bell .... paperback $9.95
THE DAKOTAS' VANISHING OUTHOUSE
 by Bruce Carlson .... paperback $9.95
VACANT LOT, SCHOOL YARD & BACK ALLEY GAMES
 by various authors .... paperback $9.95
HOW TO TALK MIDWESTERN
 by Robert Thomas .... paperback $7.95
DAKOTA COOKIN'
 by Bruce Carlson .... (3x5) paperback $5.95

ILLINOIS BOOKS

ILLINOIS COOKIN'
 by Bruce Carlson .... (3x5) paperback $5.95
THE VANISHING OUTHOUSE OF ILLINOIS
 by Bruce Carlson .... paperback $9.95
A FIELD GUIDE TO ILLINOIS' CRITTERS
 by Bruce Carlson .... paperback $7.95
YOU KNOW YOU'RE IN ILLINOIS WHEN...
 by Bruce Carlson .... paperback $7.95
Some Pretty Tame, but Kinda Funny Stories About Early
ILLINOIS LADIES-OF-THE-EVENING
 by Bruce Carlson .... paperback $9.95
ILLINOIS' ROADKILL COOKBOOK
 by Bruce Carlson .... paperback $7.95
101 WAYS TO USE A DEAD RIVER FLY
 by Bruce Carlson .... paperback $7.95

HOW TO TALK ILLINOIS
    by Netha Bell .... paperback $7.95
TALL TALES OF THE MISSISSIPPI RIVER
    by Dan Titus .... paperback $9.95
TALES OF HACKETT'S CREEK
    by Dan Titus .... paperback $9.95
UNSOLVED MYSTERIES OF THE MISSISSIPPI
    by Netha Bell .... paperback $9.95
LOST & BURIED TREASURE OF THE MISSISSIPPI RIVER
    by Netha Bell & Gary Scholl .... paperback $9.95
STRANGE FOLKS ALONG THE MISSISSIPPI
    by Pat Wallace .... paperback $9.95
LET'S US GO DOWN TO THE RIVER 'N...
    by various authors .... paperback $9.95
MISSISSIPPI RIVER PO' FOLK
    by Pat Wallace .... paperback $9.95
GHOSTS OF THE MISSISSIPPI RIVER (from Keokuk to St. Louis)
    by Bruce Carlson .... paperback $9.95
GHOSTS OF THE MISSISSIPPI RIVER (from Dubuque to Keokuk)
    by Bruce Carlson .... paperback $9.95
MAKIN' DO IN ILLINOIS
    by various authors .... paperback $9.95
MY VERY FIRST
    by various authors .... paperback $9.95
VACANT LOT, SCHOOL YARD & BACK ALLEY GAMES
    by various authors .... paperback $9.95
HOW TO TALK MIDWESTERN
    by Robert Thomas .... paperback $7.95

INDIANA BOOKS

HOW TO TALK INDIANA .... paperback $7.95
INDIANA'S ROADKILL COOKBOOK
    by Bruce Carlson .... paperback $7.95
REVENGE OF ROADKILL
    by Bruce Carlson .... paperback $7.95
A FIELD GUIDE TO SMALL INDIANA FEMALES
    by Bruce Carlson .... paperback $9.95
GHOSTS OF THE OHIO RIVER (from Cincinnati to Louisville)
    by Bruce Carlson .... paperback $9.95
LET'S US GO DOWN TO THE RIVER 'N...
    by various authors .... paperback $9.95

101 WAYS TO USE A DEAD RIVER FLY
 by Bruce Carlson .... paperback $7.95
INDIANA'S VARNISHING OUTHOUSE
 by Bruce Carlson .... paperback $9.95
VACANT LOT, SCHOOL YARD & BACK ALLEY GAMES
 by various authors .... paperback $9.95
HOW TO TALK MIDWESTERN
 by Robert Thomas .... paperback $7.95

IOWA BOOKS

IOWA COOKIN'
 by Bruce Carlson .... (3x5) paperback $5.95
IOWA'S ROADKILL COOKBOOK
 By Bruce Carlson .... paperback $7.95
REVENGE OF ROADKILL
 by Bruce Carlson .... paperback $7.95
IOWA'S OLD SCHOOLHOUSES
 by Carole Turner Johnston .... paperback $9.95
GHOSTS OF THE AMANA COLONIES
 by Lori Erickson .... paperback $9.95
GHOSTS OF THE IOWA GREAT LAKES
 by Bruce Carlson .... paperback $9.95
GHOSTS OF THE MISSISSIPPI RIVER (from Dubuque to Keokuk)
 by Bruce Carlson .... paperback $9.95
GHOSTS OF THE MISSISSIPPI RIVER (from Minneapolis to Dubuque)
 by Bruce Carlson .... paperback $9.95
GHOSTS OF POLK COUNTY, IOWA
 by Tom Welch .... paperback $9.95
TALES OF HACKETT'S CREEK
 by Dan Titus .... paperback $9.95
ME 'N WESLEY (stories about the homemade toys that
 Iowa farm children made and played with around the turn of the century)
 by Bruce Carlson .... paperback $9.95
TALL TALES OF THE MISSISSIPPI RIVER
 by Dan Titus .... paperback $9.95
HOW TO TALK IOWA .... paperback $7.95
UNSOLVED MYSTERIES OF THE MISSISSIPPI
 by Netha Bell .... paperback $9.95
101 WAYS TO USE A DEAD RIVER FLY
 by Bruce Carlson .... paperback $7.95

LET'S US GO DOWN TO THE RIVER 'N...
  by various authors .... paperback $9.95
TRICKS WE PLAYED IN IOWA
  by various authors .... paperback $9.95
IOWA, THE LAND BETWEEN THE VOWELS
  (farm boy stories from the early 1900s)
  by Bruce Carlson .... paperback $9.95
LOST & BURIED TREASURE OF THE MISSISSIPPI RIVER
  by Netha Bell & Gary Scholl .... paperback $9.95
Some Pretty Tame, but Kinda Funny Stories About Early
IOWA LADIES-OF-THE-EVENING
  by Bruce Carlson .... paperback $9.95
THE VANISHING OUTHOUSE OF IOWA
  by Bruce Carlson .... paperback $9.95
IOWA'S EARLY HOME REMEDIES
  by 26 students at Wapello Elem. School .... paperback $9.95
IOWA - A JOURNEY IN A PROMISED LAND
  by Kathy Yoder .... paperback $16.95
LOST & BURIED TREASURE OF THE MISSOURI RIVER
  by Netha Bell .... paperback $9.95
FIELD GUIDE TO IOWA'S CRITTERS
  by Bruce Carlson .... paperback $7.95
OLD IOWA HOUSES, YOUNG LOVES
  by Bruce Carlson .... paperback $9.95
SKUNK RIVER ANTHOLOGY
  by Gene Olson .... paperback $9.95
VACANT LOT, SCHOOL YARD & BACK ALLEY GAMES
  by various authors .... paperback $9.95
HOW TO TALK MIDWESTERN
  by Robert Thomas .... paperback $7.95

KANSAS BOOKS

HOW TO TALK KANSAS .... paperback $7.95
STOPOVER IN KANSAS
  by Jon McAlpin .... paperback $9.95
LET'S US GO DOWN TO THE RIVER 'N ...
  by various authors .... paperback $9.95
LOST & BURIED TREASURE OF THE MISSOURI RIVER
  by Netha Bell .... paperback $9.95

101 WAYS TO USE A DEAD RIVER FLY
 by Bruce Carlson .... paperback $7.95
VACANT LOT, SCHOOL YARD & BACK ALLEY GAMES
 by various authors .... paperback $9.95
HOW TO TALK MIDWESTERN
 by Robert Thomas .... paperback $7.95

KENTUCKY BOOKS

GHOSTS OF THE OHIO RIVER (from Pittsburgh to Cincinnati)
 by Bruce Carlson .... paperback $9.95
GHOSTS OF THE OHIO RIVER (from Cincinnati to Louisville)
 by Bruce Carlson .... paperback $9.95
TALES OF HACKETT'S CREEK
 by Dan Titus .... paperback $9.95
LOST & BURIED TREASURE OF THE MISSISSIPPI RIVER
 by Netha Bell & Gary Scholl .... paperback $9.95
LET'S US GO DOWN TO THE RIVER 'N ...
 by various authors .... paperback $9.95
UNSOLVED MYSTERIES OF THE MISSISSIPPI
 by Netha Bell .... paperback $9.95
101 WAYS TO USE A DEAD RIVER FLY
 by Bruce Carlson .... paperback $7.95
TALL TALES OF THE MISSISSIPPI RIVER
 by Dan Titus .... paperback $9.95
MY VERY FIRST
 by various authors .... paperback $9.95
VACANT LOT, SCHOOL YARD & BACK ALLEY GAMES
 by various authors .... paperback $9.95

MICHIGAN BOOKS

MICHIGAN COOKIN'
 by Bruce Carlson .... (3x5) paperback $5.95
MICHIGAN'S ROADKILL COOKBOOK
 by Bruce Carlson .... paperback $7.95
MICHIGAN'S VANISHING OUTHOUSE
 by Bruce Carlson .... paperback $9.95

MINNESOTA BOOKS

MINNESOTA'S ROADKILL COOKBOOK
    by Bruce Carlson .... paperback $7.95
REVENGE OF ROADKILL
    by Bruce Carlson .... paperback $7.95
A FIELD GUIDE TO SMALL MINNESOTA FEMALES
    by Bruce Carlson .... paperback $9.95
GHOSTS OF THE MISSISSIPPI RIVER (from Minneapolis to Dubuque)
    by Bruce Carlson .... paperback $9.95
LAKES COUNTRY COOKBOOK
    by Bruce Carlson .... paperback $11.95
UNSOLVED MYSTERIES OF THE MISSISSIPPI
    by Netha Bell .... paperback $9.95
TALES OF HACKETT'S CREEK
    by Dan Titus .... paperback $9.95
GHOSTS OF SOUTHWEST MINNESOTA
    by Ruth Hein .... paperback $9.95
HOW TO TALK LIKE A MINNESOTA NATIVE .... paperback $7.95
MINNESOTA'S VANISHING OUTHOUSE
    by Bruce Carlson .... paperback $9.95
TALL TALES OF THE MISSISSIPPI RIVER
    by Dan Titus .... paperback $9.95
Some Pretty Tame, but Kinda Funny Stories About Early
MINNESOTA LADIES-OF-THE-EVENING
    by Bruce Carlson .... paperback $9.95
101 WAYS TO USE A DEAD RIVER FLY .... paperback $7.95
LOST & BURIED TREASURE OF THE MISSISSIPPI RIVER
    by Netha Bell & Gary Scholl .... paperback $9.95
VACANT LOT, SCHOOL YARD & BACK ALLEY GAMES
    · by various authors .... paperback $9.95
HOW TO TALK MIDWESTERN
    by Robert Thomas .... paperback $7.95
MINNESOTA COOKIN'
    by Bruce Carlson .... (3x5) paperback $5.95

MISSOURI BOOKS

MISSOURI COOKIN'
    by Bruce Carlson .... (3x5) paperback $5.95
MISSOURI'S ROADKILL COOKBOOK
    by Bruce Carlson .... paperback $7.95

REVENGE OF ROADKILL
 by Bruce Carlson .... paperback $7.95
LET'S US GO DOWN TO THE RIVER 'N ...
 by various authors .... paperback $9.95
LAKES COUNTRY COOKBOOK
 by Bruce Carlson .... paperback $11.95
101 WAYS TO USE A DEAD RIVER FLY
 by Bruce Carlson .... paperback $7.95
TALL TALES OF THE MISSISSIPPI RIVER
 by Dan Titus .... paperback $9.95
TALES OF HACKETT'S CREEK
 by Dan Titus .... paperback $9.95
STRANGE FOLKS ALONG THE MISSISSIPPI
 by Pat Wallace .... paperback $9.95
LOST & BURIED TREASURE OF THE MISSOURI RIVER
 by Netha Bell .... paperback $9.95
HOW TO TALK MISSOURIAN
 by Bruce Carlson .... paperback $7.95
VACANT LOT, SCHOOL YARD & BACK ALLEY GAMES
 by various authors .... paperback $9.95
HOW TO TALK MIDWESTERN
 by Robert Thomas .... paperback $7.95
UNSOLVED MYSTERIES OF THE MISSISSIPPI
 by Netha Bell .... paperback $9.95
LOST & BURIED TREASURE OF THE MISSISSIPPI RIVER
 by Netha Bell & Gary Scholl .... paperback $9.95
MISSISSIPPI RIVER PO' FOLK
 by Pat Wallace .... paperback $9.95
Some Pretty Tame, but Kinda Funny Stories About Early
MISSOURI LADIES-OF-THE-EVENING
 by Bruce Carlson .... paperback $9.95
GUNSHOOTIN', WHISKEY DRINKIN', GIRL CHASIN'
STORIES OUT OF THE OLD MISSOURI TERRITORY
 by Bruce Carlson .... paperback $9.95
THE VANISHING OUTHOUSE OF MISSOURI
 by Bruce Carlson .... paperback $9.95
A FIELD GUIDE TO MISSOURI'S CRITTERS
 by Bruce Carlson .... paperback $7.95
EARLY MISSOURI HOME REMEDIES
 by various authors .... paperback $9.95
GHOSTS OF THE OZARKS
 by Bruce Carlson .... paperback $9.95

MISSISSIPPI RIVER COOKIN' BOOK
 by Bruce Carlson .... paperback $11.95
MISSOURI'S OLD HOUSES, AND NEW LOVES
 by Bruce Carlson .... paperback $9.95
UNDERGROUND MISSOURI
 by Bruce Carlson .... paperback $9.95

NEBRASKA BOOKS

LOST & BURIED TREASURE OF THE MISSOURI RIVER
 by Netha Bell .... paperback $9.95
101 WAYS TO USE A DEAD RIVER FLY
 by Bruce Carlson .... paperback $7.95
LET'S US GO DOWN TO THE RIVER 'N ...
 by various authors .... paperback $9.95
HOW TO TALK MIDWESTERN
 by Robert Thomas .... paperback $7.95
VACANT LOT, SCHOOL YARD & BACK ALLEY GAMES
 by various authors .... paperback $9.95

TENNESSEE BOOKS

TALES OF HACKETT'S CREED
 by Dan Titus .... paperback $9.95
TALL TALES OF THE MISSISSIPPI RIVER
 by Dan Titus .... paperback $9.95
UNSOLVED MYSTERIES OF THE MISSISSIPPI
 by Netha Bell .... paperback $9.95
LOST & BURIED TREASURE OF THE MISSISSIPPI RIVER
 by Netha Bell & Gary Scholl .... paperback $9.95
LET'S US GO DOWN TO THE RIVER 'N ...
 by various authors .... paperback $9.95
101 WAYS TO USE A DEAD RIVER FLY
 by Bruce Carlson .... paperback $7.95
VACANT LOT, SCHOOL YARD & BACK ALLEY GAMES
 by various authors .... paperback $9.95

WISCONSIN BOOKS

HOW TO TALK WISCONSIN .... paperback $7.95
WISCONSIN COOKIN'
    by Bruce Carlson .... (3x5) paperback $5.95
WISCONSIN'S ROADKILL COOKBOOK
    by Bruce Carlson .... paperback $7.95
REVENGE OF ROADKILL
    by Bruce Carlson .... paperback $7.95
TALL TALES OF THE MISSISSIPPI RIVER
    by Dan Titus .... paperback $9.95
LAKES COUNTRY COOKBOOK
    by Bruce Carlson .... paperback $11.95
TALES OF HACKETT'S CREEK
    by Dan Titus .... paperback $9.95
LET'S US GO DOWN TO THE RIVER 'N ...
    by various authors .... paperback $9.95
101 WAYS TO USE A DEAD RIVER FLY
    by Bruce Carlson .... paperback $7.95
UNSOLVED MYSTERIES OF THE MISSISSIPPI
    by Netha Bell .... paperback $9.95
LOST & BURIED TREASURE OF THE MISSISSIPPI RIVER
    by Netha Bell & Gary Scholl .... paperback $9.95
GHOSTS OF THE MISSISSIPPI RIVER (from Dubuque to Keokuk)
    by Bruce Carlson .... paperback $9.95
HOW TO TALK MIDWESTERN
    by Robert Thomas .... paperback $7.95
VACANT LOT, SCHOOL YARD & BACK ALLEY GAMES
    by various authors .... paperback $9.95
MY VERY FIRST
    by various authors .... paperback $9.95
EARLY WISCONSIN HOME REMEDIES
    by various authors .... paperback $9.95
GHOSTS OF THE MISSISSIPPI RIVER (from Minneapolis to Dubuque)
    by Bruce Carlson .... paperback $9.95
THE VANISHING OUTHOUSE OF WISCONSIN
    by Bruce Carlson .... paperback $9.95
GHOSTS OF DOOR COUNTY, WISCONSIN
    by Geri Rider .... paperback $9.95
Some Pretty Tame, but Kinda Funny Stories About Early
WISCONSIN LADIES-OF-THE-EVENING
    by Bruce Carlson .... paperback $9.95

MIDWESTERN BOOKS

A FIELD GUIDE TO THE MIDWEST'S WORST RESTAURANTS
by Bruce Carlson .... paperback $5.95
THE MOTORIST'S FIELD GUIDE TO MIDWESTERN FARM
EQUIPMENT (misguided information as only a city slicker can give it)
by Bruce Carlson .... paperback $5.95
VACANT LOT, SCHOOL YARD & BACK ALLEY GAMES
OF THE MIDWEST YEARS AGO
by various authors .... paperback $9.95
MIDWEST SMALL TOWN COOKING
by Bruce Carlson .... (3x5) paperback $5.95
HITCHHIKING THE UPPER MIDWEST
by Bruce Carlson .... paperback $7.95
101 WAYS FOR MIDWESTERNERS TO "DO IN" THEIR
NEIGHBOR'S PESKY DOG WITHOUT GETTING CAUGHT
by Bruce Carlson .... paperback $5.95

RIVER BOOKS

ON THE SHOULDERS OF A GIANT
by M. Cody and D. Walker .... paperback $9.95
SKUNK RIVER ANTHOLOGY
by Gene "Will" Olson .... paperback $9.95
JACK KING vs. DETECTIVE MACKENZIE
by Netha Bell .... paperback $9.95
LOST & BURIED TREASURES ALONG THE MISSISSIPPI
by Netha Bell & Gary Scholl .... paperback $9.95
MISSISSIPPI RIVER PO' FOLK
by Pat Wallace .... paperback $9.95
STRANGE FOLKS ALONG THE MISSISSIPPI
by Pat Wallace .... paperback $9.95
GHOSTS OF THE OHIO RIVER (from Pittsburgh to Cincinnati)
by Bruce Carlson .... paperback $9.95
GHOSTS OF THE OHIO RIVER (from Cincinnati to Louisville)
by Bruce Carlson .... paperback $9.95
GHOSTS OF THE MISSISSIPPI RIVER (Minneapolis to Dubuque)
by Bruce Carlson .... paperback $9.95
GHOSTS OF THE MISSISSIPPI RIVER (Dubuque to Keokuk)
by Bruce Carlson .... paperback $9.95
TALL TALES OF THE MISSISSIPPI RIVER
by Dan Titus .... paperback $9.95

TALL TALES OF THE MISSOURI RIVER
　　　by Dan Titus .... paperback $9.95
RIVER SHARKS & SHENANIGANS
　(tales of riverboat gambling of years ago)
　　　by Netha Bell .... paperback $9.95
UNSOLVED MYSTERIES OF THE MISSISSIPPI
　　　by Netha Bell .... paperback $9.95
TALES OF HACKETT'S CREEK (1940s Mississippi River kids)
　　　by Dan Titus .... paperback $9.95
101 WAYS TO USE A DEAD RIVER FLY
　　　by Bruce Carlson .... paperback $7.95
LET'S US GO DOWN TO THE RIVER 'N ...
　　　by various authors .... paperback $9.95
LOST & BURIED TREASURE OF THE MISSOURI
　　　by Netha Bell .... paperback $9.95

COOKBOOKS

ROARING 20's COOKBOOK
　　　by Bruce Carlson .... paperback $11.95
DEPRESSION COOKBOOK
　　　by Bruce Carlson .... paperback $11.95
LAKES COUNTRY COOKBOOK
　　　by Bruce Carlson .... paperback $11.95
A COOKBOOK FOR THEM WHAT AIN'T DONE A LOT OF COOKIN'
　　　by Bruce Carlson .... paperback $11.95
FLAT-OUT DIRT-CHEAP COOKIN' COOKBOOK
　　　by Bruce Carlson .... paperback $11.95
APHRODISIAC COOKING
　　　by Bruce Carlson .... paperback $11.95
WILD CRITTER COOKBOOK
　　　by Bruce Carlson .... paperback $11.95
I GOT FUNNIER-THINGS-TO-DO-THAN-COOKIN' COOKBOOK
　　　by Louise Lum .... paperback $11.95
MISSISSIPPI RIVER COOKIN' BOOK
　　　by Bruce Carlson .... paperback $11.95
HUNTING IN THE NUDE COOKBOOK
　　　by Bruce Carlson .... paperback $9.95
DAKOTA COOKIN'
　　　by Bruce Carlson .... (3x5) paperback $5.95
IOWA COOKIN'
　　　by Bruce Carlson .... (3x5) paperback $5.95

MICHIGAN COOKIN'
	by Bruce Carlson .... (3x5) paperback $5.95
MINNESOTA COOKIN'
	by Bruce Carlson .... (3x5) paperback $5.95
MISSOURI COOKIN'
	by Bruce Carlson .... (3x5) paperback $5.95
ILLINOIS COOKIN'
	by Bruce Carlson .... (3x5) paperback $5.95
WISCONSIN COOKIN'
	by Bruce Carlson .... (3x5) paperback $5.95
HILL COUNTRY COOKIN'
	by Bruce Carlson .... (3x5) paperback $5.95
MIDWEST SMALL TOWN COOKIN'
	by Bruce Carlson .... (3x5) paperback $5.95
APHRODISIAC COOKIN'
	by Bruce Carlson .... (3x5) paperback $5.95
PREGNANT LADY COOKIN'
	by Bruce Carlson .... (3x5) paperback $5.95
GOOD COOKIN' FROM THE PLAIN PEOPLE
	by Bruce Carlson .... (3x5) paperback $5.95
WORKING GIRL COOKING
	by Bruce Carlson .... (3x5) paperback $5.95
COOKING FOR ONE
	by Barb Layton .... paperback $11.95
SUPER SIMPLE COOKING
	by Barb Layton .... (3x5) paperback $5.95
OFF TO COLLEGE COOKBOOK
	by Barb Layton .... (3x5) paperback $5.95
COOKING WITH THINGS THAT GO SPLASH
	by Bruce Carlson .... (3x5) paperback $5.95
COOKING WITH THINGS THAT GO MOO
	by Bruce Carlson .... (3x5) paperback $5.95
COOKING WITH SPIRITS
	by Bruce Carlson .... (3x5) paperback $5.95
INDIAN COOKING COOKBOOK
	by Bruce Carlson .... paperback $9.95
DIAL-A-DREAM COOKBOOK
	by Bruce Carlson .... (3x5) paperback $5.95
HORMONE HELPER COOKBOOK .... (3x5) paperback $5.95

MISCELLANEOUS BOOKS

DEAR TABBY (letters to and from a feline advice columnist)
 by Bruce Carlson .... paperback $5.95
HOW TO BEHAVE (etiquette advice for non-traditional
and awkward circumstances such as attending dogfights,
what to do when your blind date turns out to be your spouse, etc.)
 by Bruce Carlson .... paperback $5.95
REVENGE OF THE ROADKILL
 by Bruce Carlson .... paperback $7.95